FIRENZE
MVSEI

The Uffizi

Gloria Fossi

GIUNTI

Graphics: Franco Bulletti
Cover design: Laura Belforte *and* Fabio Filippi

Managing editor: Claudio Pescio
Editing: Augusta Tosone
Translation: Harriet Paterson, Marina Pugliano *and* Catherine Frost

Photographs: Giunti Archive / Photo Rabatti-Domingie, Florence;
Soprintendenza Speciale PSAE-PMCF / Sergio Garbari Photo

www.giunti.it

Via Bolognese 165 - 50139 Florence - Italy
Via Dante 4 - 20121 Milan - Italy

First edition: October 1998
Updated edition: November 2010

Reprint	Year
6 5 4 3 2	2015 2014 2013 2012

Printed by Giunti Industrie Grafiche S.p.A. – Prato

Contents

MICHELANGELO, *Doni Tondo* (detail)

ENOUGH BOOKS have been written about the public museums in Florence run by the Superintendence for Florentine Museum Center to fill a large library. This is hardly surprising when one considers that the artistic heritage preserved in our museums has been famous throughout the world for centuries. For hundreds of years writers, scholars and travellers of every nationality and country have been attempting to describe all that the Florentine museums contain. They have made great efforts to explain why these museums are so fascinating, and to lead a path through paintings and sculptures for both the uninformed but willing visitor and the refined and jaded intellectual.

Over time, however, the museums have altered their aspect and their layout, the exhibitions have been arranged in new ways, the collections have been enriched (or impoverished). Attributions of works in the museums have also changed, restorations have transformed the appearance of many pieces, the rise and fall of aesthetic tendencies have led to reorganisation and the exhibition of differing works. All these things are constantly taking place within the public collections because museology and the history of art, like any intellectual endeavour, are in a constant state of progress and transformation. This explains why the literature surrounding the Florentine museums (like that of any of the world's great art collections) is so immense, and in a process of continual updating and change.

The perfect, definitive guide to a museum, any museum, does not and cannot exist.

The premise seems obvious, but is nonetheless necessary in order to understand the point of the publication introduced by these lines. From the moment when, in accordance with the application of the Ronchey law 4/93, the Giunti publishing house group took over the running of the support services within the Florentine museum system, it was decided to start at once on a standardised series of illustrated guides. These guides, displaying the cuneiform flower of "Firenze Musei" *on the cover, guarantee that at the year of publication the state of each museum is exactly that described in the guide.*

Certain things are obviously necessary if a museum guide is to aspire to reliability, official standing and at the same time enjoy a wide distribution: accuracy of information, high quality reproductions, an easily manageable format, a reasonable cost and – not least – a clearly written text (without, naturally, being banal or lacking in precision). Readers will judge for themselves if the guide which follows this introduction reaches these standards. I have no doubt that this will be a serious and committed judgement, just as myself and the Publisher of this guide have been serious and committed in attempting to meet the cultural needs of whoever visits our museums in the best way and with every possible care.

Antonio Paolucci

Sandro Botticelli, *Pallas and the Centaur*

The Uffizi: its Origins and Collections

One of the world's most important museums, the Uffizi Gallery was one of the first in Europe to emerge in accordance with the modern idea of a museum, that is to say as a systematically organised exhibition space designed for public viewing. Two centuries before it was officially opened in 1765, the Gallery was in fact open to visitors on request: in 1591, a guide to Florence written by Francesco Bocchi describes it as: "amongst the most supremely beautiful sights... in the World... filled with ancient statues, with noble paintings and extremely precious objects". It is worth remembering that it was created in a city which had long since been the first to revisit the disused term *museum*, which for the ancient Greeks signified a space dedicated to the Muses: in Florence it was used to describe the collection of antique sculptures which Lorenzo the Magnificent (1449-1492) established in the garden at San Marco. Artists such as Leonardo and Michelangelo gathered here "for beauty, for work and for recreation", as Giorgio Vasari relates. This latter was not only the architect of the Uffizi but also the author of the *Lives of the Artists* published in 1550 and in 1568, a work which will frequently be referred to in this guide.

The origins of the Uffizi date back to 1560, when at the request of the Medici duke Cosimo I (1519-1574), Vasari designed a grand *palazzo* with two wings, "along the river, almost floating in the air", which housed the *Magistrature*, or the administrative and judicial offices – *Uffizi* – of the duchy of Tuscany. Five years later Vasari oversaw in a few short months the building of the elevated gallery which, connecting the Uffizi to the new Medici residence at Palazzo Pitti, runs to this day over the Ponte Vecchio and the church of Santa Felicita, leading out into the Boboli gardens. In a unique urban relationship, the Vasari Corridor unites the nerve centres of city: the river, the oldest bridge and the seats of power, along a spectacular elevated walkway.

But it is to Cosimo's son, Francesco I (1541-1587) that we owe the first real nucleus of the Gallery. The introverted Grand Duke had already established a Studiolo filled with paintings and precious objects in his residence in the Palazzo Vecchio, which was later also joined to the Uffizi by an elevated passageway. Around 1581 he transformed the top floor of the Uffizi into a gallery, a place for "walking, with paintings, statues and other precious things", and in 1586 gave the eclectic Bernardo Buontalenti the task of creating the Medici Theatre. This provided a space for memorable performances, and corresponded in height to the present first and second floors of the museum, where we now find the col-

The Medici Theatre on the first floor

lections of graphic works and other exhibition rooms. The Gallery was illuminated by large windows, decorated by antique sculptures and by frescoes on the ceiling. But the most creative idea was the Tribune: a symbolic, unusual, welcoming space, its octagonal cupola encrusted with shells, filled with works of art and furnishings, all lit from above. Near the Tribune is a terrace which was closed in by the Grand Duke Ferdinand, brother of Francesco, in 1589, to create the Loggia of Geographical Maps (Room 16). At the end of the other wing a hanging garden was created over Orcagna's Loggia, beyond the Foundry and other workshops.

Nowadays the Uffizi Gallery boasts an incomparable artistic heritage: thousands of pictures from the medieval to the modern age, ancient sculptures, miniatures, tapestries; it holds an unrivalled position for its series of self-portraits which is constantly growing through acquisitions and through donations by contemporary artists, equalled only by its collection in the Cabinet of Drawings and Prints, outstanding even for this city which traditionally prides itself on being "pre-eminent in drawing".

If the Uffizi Gallery can rightly be called a museum *par excellence*, this is not just because of its superb buildings and its works of art. Its unique quality also comes from the origins of its collections, from its history which goes back more than four centuries and which is so closely entwined with the events of Florentine civilisation. That the Uffizi is a byword for Florence and vice-versa is explained above all by the inborn vocation for collecting of its governors, with the Medicis

View of the Loggia of the Uffizi over the Arno

leading the way: the lords of Florence for three centuries, they were also passionate patrons and collectors of antiquities from the time of Cosimo the Elder (1389-1464) who was the patron of artists such as the transgressive Fra Filippo Lippi (Room 8).

The first Medicean collections form, as mentioned earlier, the original nucleus of the Gallery. However it is also true, as the reader of this guide will realise from the provenances catalogued here, that many works of art destined for other locations which eventually found their way to this great U-shaped building in the heart of the city reflect the tastes and choices of public figures and private citizens, of merchants, bankers and *literati* as well as of civic and religious institutions. One need only mention, in connection with the early 15th century, the cultured and vastly wealthy Palla Strozzi, who approached Gentile da Fabriano, a stranger in Florence, for an *Adoration* for his chapel in Santa Trinita: a work which in its exotic magic is a long way from the simple, essential world being evoked in those years by the Tuscan artist Masaccio. This latter worked with Masolino for the powerful Felice Brancacci, and before that for the religious sisters of Sant'Ambrogio (Room 7).

In the 16th century one should at least mention Agnolo Doni, patron of Michelangelo (Room 25) and also of Raphael, to whom he was as important a patron as Lorenzo Nasi (Room 26); and Bartolomeo Panciatichi, painted together with his extremely beautiful wife by Bronzino (Tribune). The Florentine guilds were also important patrons during the 14th and 15th centuries;

A window of the Vasari Corridor over the Arno

amongst these were the Bankers Guild, who commissioned a triptych from Orcagna for the pillar on its property in Orsanmichele, the seat of the Arts (Room 4), and the Merchants' Guild, who asked Piero Pollaiolo and then Botticelli for a series of *Virtues* for its Tribunal (Room 9). Lastly, many works now in the Gallery exist thanks to the patronage of the churches, confraternities and monasteries in and around Florence, from which, furthermore, various artist-monks emerged such as Fra Angelico, Lorenzo Monaco and Fra Bartolomeo (Rooms 5-6, 7, 25).

There are other historical considerations which add to the unique nature of the Uffizi's collections: since the 14th century Florence has had a closely-woven international network which has led, often through indirect routes, to fruitful exchange with foreign artistic influences: the Portinari, agents of the Medici in Bruges, sent the imposing Van der Goes triptych to the church of Sant'Egidio (Rooms 10-14), and had themselves painted by the Flemish Memling (Room 22). In addition, official visits by dignitaries and high-ranking prelates almost always brought some artistic novelty or other to the banks of the Arno: a chapel in San Miniato was dedicated to the Cardinal of Portugal who died in Florence in 1459, and it was from this chapel that the magnificent altarpiece of Pollaiolo (Room 9) came. For the marriage of Maria de' Medici to Henri IV (1600), the Vicenzan Filippo Pigafetta (1533-1604) published a description of the Gallery for strangers to the city and planned a room of military architecture (Room 17). Diplomatic gifts, dowries and inheritances from international marriages en-

Wrestlers, copy from a Greek original in bronze, Tribune

larged the collections of the grand dukes, who were developing more and more of a taste for works from other Italian and foreign schools and contemporary, non-Florentine artists. A few examples: Ferdinand I (1549-1609), who had already acquired in Rome in 1583 the famous and only recently discovered antique sculptural group of the *Wrestlers* (in the Tribune since 1677), received as a gift from Cardinal del Monte the *Medusa* by Caravaggio (Room 43) and inherited miniatures and other works from his wife Christine of Lorraine, granddaughter of Caterina de' Medici. Ferdinand II (1610-1670) inherited through his wife Vittoria della Rovere the Piero della Francesca *Diptych* (Room 8) and Titian's *Venus of Urbino* (Room 28), amongst other things, and acquired Nordic paintings through the artist Agostino Tassi, the Medici's first artistic intermediary. Cosimo II (1590-1621) was an admirer of the Emilian Guercino as was his son, the erudite Cardinal Leopoldo (1617-1675), who founded the Accademia del Cimento, and formed the first collections of self-portraits and drawings. Cosimo III (1642-1723) bought foreign paintings, particularly Flemish ones, such as the two great canvases of Rubens damaged by the 1993 bomb, now restored. And finally the Grand Prince Ferdinand (1663-1713) invited artists like Giuseppe Maria Crespi, Magnasco and the two Riccis to Florence. When the Medici dynasty died out, the last heir Anna Maria Luisa (1667-1743) sanctioned the Gallery as "public and inalienable property", granting the Uffizi a new lease of life during the Grand Duchy of Lorraine, especially under the enlightened figure of Pietro Leopoldo (Grand Duke of Tuscany from 1765 to 1790),

WORKSHOP OF FRANÇOIS CLOUET, *Henri II, Caterina de' Medici and relatives*, c. 1570

to whom we owe the entrance stairways, the vestibule and the Niobe Room. A renewed taste for primitives led to the acquisition of earlier works, which often came from suppressed convents and monasteries; the nucleus of French painting was formed at that time and the first "scientific" guides were published (Bencivenni Pelli, 1779; Luigi Lanzi, 1782).

From the 19th century onwards, the growth of the picture gallery has brought about new displays and new rooms, a process which, despite changing circumstances, has been almost uninterrupted to this day, notwithstanding the bomb of 1993. During the postwar period, various rearrangements and restorations have been carried out by Roberto Salvini, Luisa Becherucci and Luciano Berti. Many other high-profile interventions have taken place since 1987 under the current director Annamaria Petrioli Tofani, who alongside the conservators Giovanni Agosti, Caterina Caneva, Alessandro Cecchi, Antonio Natali, Piera Bocci Pacini and the architect Antonio Godoli, has carried out the restoration of the Royal Postroom on the ground floor, of various exhibition rooms and of the Loggia on the first floor; the philological restoration of the Gallery's three corridors and the reorganisation following new criteria of many of the rooms (8 and 15 in the eastern wing and most of the rooms in the west wing). Since March 2004 woork has been proceeding to extend the museum into the vast areas beneath the Gallery is now at hand, which will include the creation of service areas. Owing to an improved layout of tapestries, paintings and other works from the museum's deposits – with consequent changes and altered positions for

G. NASINI, *Virtues of the Medici Grand Dukes*, c. 1698. Ceiling of the Second Corridor

works already on display, particularly for the 17th and 18th century paintings which until now were cramped in the last room of the Third corridor – it will be possible to trace an ever-more meaningful art-historical journey through schools and eras. The remarkable Contini Bonacossi collection, previously in the Meridiana pavillion at Palazzo Pitti, has also finally been given a definitive display; there is a temporary entrance from Via Lambertesca but the collection will soon be linked directly to the rest of the museum. In addition, the spectacular Loggia on the Arno (corresponding to the Gallery's Southern Corridor), which opened in December 1998, is an integral part of the new Uffizi.

NOTE

The Uffizi Gallery is undergoing a phase of large-scale enlargement and reorganisation. The extension of the exhibition space on the First Floor of the building may cause the temporary closure of some rooms, and the repositioning of certain works, at times which it is not presently possible to predict. The collections of paintings from the seventeenth and eighteenth century will be subject to extensive reorganisation.
Measurements are given in centimetres unless otherwise indicated. The inventory numbers, unless otherwise specified, refer to those taken from the Inventario generale delle Gallerie fiorentine, *known to scholars as* Inventario 1890.

The Hall of San Pier Scheraggio

Erected over the foundation of a 9th century church and consecrated in 1068, the church of San Pier Scheraggio was until 1313 the seat of the town councils and the site of memorable public speeches by Dante and Boccaccio. Some of the arches of the left nave, which was destroyed in 1410 to enlarge Via della Ninna, are still visible from the exterior. Among the remaining medieval structures, incorporated into the ground floor of the Uffizi in 1560, the central nave still stands, which since 1971 has been restored and converted into an impressive two-roomed exhibition space. Of note amongst the works on display here, which include decorative fragments from the Roman and Medieval ages, is Andrea del Castagno's cycle of humanistic frescoes. This work was recovered in 1847 from Villa Carducci, later to become Villa Pandolfini. In it the social status of characters from recent Florentine history is reflected by depicting them together with heroic figures from the Bible and antiquity.

Andrea del Castagno

Queen Tomyris

c. 1449-1450
Detached fresco
transferred to canvas
245×155
Inv. San Marco e Cenacoli
no. 168
In the Uffizi since 1969

In his *Memoriale* of 1510, Francesco Albertini records that Andrea del Castagno painted a "most beautiful" loggia, with "Sibyls and famous Florentine men", for Gonfalonier Carducci's villa in Legnaia, on the outskirts of Florence.
The cycle's decorative fragments include the Cumaean Sibyl, the ancient heroines Queens Esther and Tomyris, and six famous Florentines. The figures are almost sculptural in form-standing out against feigned panels they create an effect of three-dimensional space around them.

Andrea del Castagno
Pippo Spano

c. 1449-1450
Detached fresco transferred to canvas, 250×154
Inv. San Marco e Cenacoli no. 173
In the Uffizi since 1969

Pippo Spano (so-called after the title *ispán* of Temesvár that he received in 1407), otherwise known as Filippo Scolari, was a Hungarian with Florentine origins, a brave army leader who fought against the Bosnians, and a capable diplomat under Siegmund of Bohemia who named him governor of Bosnia. This fresco portrays Spano with an appearance close to the description left to us by Jacopo di Poggio Bracciolini: "Black-eyed, white-haired, merry of face, thin in body. He wore a long beard and hair down to his shoulders".

Andrea del Castagno
Francesco Petrarca

c. 1449-1450
Detached fresco transferred to canvas, 247×153
Inv. San Marco e Cenacoli no. 166
In the Uffizi since 1969

In the cycle of famous Florentines at Villa Carducci, the portrait of the poet Petrarch together with those of Dante and Boccaccio represents the virtues of literature.

Archaeological Collections

The exhibition of the prestigious Medicean collection of antiquities originally came from the Sculpture Gallery of Francesco I in the First Corridor, along which each statue alternated symmetrically with two busts of Roman emperors. This gallery also included several works now in other museums: "modern" sculptures such as Michelangelo's Bacchus, *Etruscan pieces such as the* Chimera *and* Orator *previously acquired by Cosimo I, and in addition the* Wild Boar *(now in the Third Corridor) and the* Dying Alexander *(now in the Second Corridor). The collection increased between the 17*[th] *and the 18*[th] *centuries, mainly due to the arrival of works from the Villa Medici in Rome such as the* Medici Venus, *the* Knife-Grinder *and the* Wrestlers *(Tribune), and finally the* Niobe Group. *Dozens of pieces are now redistributed between Room 1 (1981 arrangement), the Tribune, the three Corridors (1996 arrangement), the Niobe Room, the Vestibules, and the Loggia on the Arno, all following the original display as closely as possible. Of the various works found in Room 1, of particular note is the Roman copy in green basalt of the* Doryphorus *torso of Polykleitos. Also originally from the Villa Medici, it has been in the Uffizi since 1783.*

Bust of Antinous

Roman art
from the time of Hadrian
Greek marble
h. 80
Inv. no. 327

Discovered in Rome in 1671, this bust comes from the collection of Cardinal Leopoldo de' Medici. Considered to be the last mythical interpretation of Greek Art, it represents an idealised portrait of the young Bithynian, favourite of the Emperor Hadrian.

Boy Removing a Thorn from his Foot

Roman copy, Augustan period, from the Greek original (modern head and other additions)
Pentelic marble, h. 84
Inv. no. 177

Originally from the Villa Medici in Rome, this ancient marble sculpture was transferred from the Villa di Poggio Imperiale to the Uffizi in 1772. The boy removing a thorn from his foot is an image which, known and copied several times in Rome from the 12th century, began from the 15th century onwards to interest Renaissance Florentine artists who copied and adapted it for religious scenes.

Cabinet of Prints and Drawings

The traditional gift of Florentine artists for drawing dates back to at least the time of Cennino Cennini, a painter as well as the author of a treatise on artistic techniques, who at in the beginning of the 15th century considered drawing "the foundation of art". A further significant claim was then made in the 16th century by the great draftsman Pontormo, who considered drawing to be the noblest form of expression. One of the first people to value drawing as a separate art was Giorgio Vasari, fervent collector, capable draftsman, and an expert on technique. Since the time of Lorenzo the Medici had also collected drawings, but it was under Cardinal Leopoldo (1617-1675) that the true beginnings of the Uffizi collection, then in the Pitti, were laid down. Today this is the most outstanding collection of graphic work in Italy, and one of the most important in the world: it boasts works of fundamental importance from the 14th-15th centuries to the present day, and contains works by great masters such as Leonardo, Michelangelo, Raphael, Andrea del Sarto, Pontormo and many others. The rooms it currently occupies while waiting for future enlargements are on the first floor, in areas created from the 16th century Medici Theatre. The works are only on view for the purposes of study, but themed exhibitions are periodically open to the public.

Leonardo da Vinci
Landscape

Dated on the top left corner: "dì di Santa Maria della neve addì 5 d'aghossto 1473"
Pen on yellowed white paper
mm 196×287
Inv. G.D.S.U. no. 8 P r.
From the Fondo Mediceo Lorenese

This is the first known dated work of Leonardo's and the first drawing of pure landscape in western art. It dates back, as indicated by Leonardo's mirror writing, to the day of the miraculous summer snowfall on the Esquiline Hill in Rome. Possibly showing the Arno valley as viewed from the mountainside of Montalbano, the drawing witnesses to Leonardo's interest in nature.

Raphael
Nude Study

c. 1509
Charcoal and white chalk on yellowed white paper
mm 357×210
Inv. G.D.S.U. no. 541 E r.

This was the preparatory drawing for the figure of Adam in the fresco of the *Disputation over the Sacrament* in Raphael's Stanza della Segnatura (1509) in the Vatican.
An outstanding draftsman, the vigorous lines with which he sketches this almost sculptural nude show that he had studied the work of Michelangelo as well as antique sculpture; it comes as little surprise that in 1515 Raphael was named Head of of Roman Antiquities by the Medici pope, Leo X.

First Corridor

After a restoration in 1996, the East Corridor (illustrated below) has largely recovered its late 16th century appearance, conceived by Francesco I, founder of the Gallery. The restoration of the corridor and its display of statues and paintings is based amongst other things upon the drawings of the Gallery carried out by Fra Benedetto de Greyss between 1748 and 1765. Following the categories defined in 1597 by Filippo Pigafetta, the older portraits from the Giovio Series, partly restored, have been placed under the ceiling, which is decorated with grotesque *motifs. The series depicts famous men from every age and country, and was begun for Cosimo I by Cristofano dell'Altissimo, who in Como (1552-1589) copied the renowned collection by Paolo Giovio. They then passed from the Pitti Palace to the Uffizi in 1587. After more than two centuries, the large three-quarter-length portraits of the Aulic series are now set back in regular spaces beneath the Giovio Series. Francesco I and his successors commissioned these to extol their family, beginning with the founder, Giovanni di Bicci. They were inspired by older prototypes, some of which are still in the Tribune. Ancient busts and sculptures from the Medici collection alternate along the walls. The ceilings with* grotesque *decoration were executed by a group of painters led by Alessandro Allori (Antonio Tempesta, Ludovico Buti, Giovan Maria Butteri and Ludovico Cigoli, some of whom were already active in the Studiolo of Palazzo Vecchio). The pavement in large white and grey marble squares dates back to the Lorraine period (18th century).*

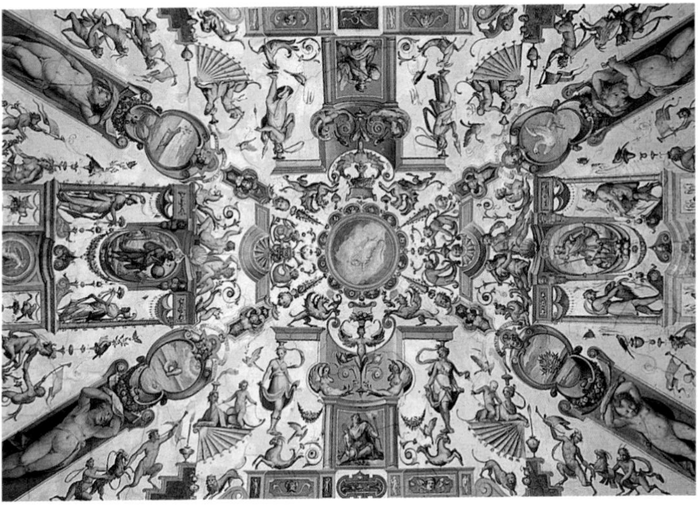

ALESSANDRO ALLORI
Grotesque Decorations with Medicean Devices

1581
Fresco with tempera retouches
385×585

The *grotesque*, a typical decoration inspired by the friezes in imperial Roman residences, takes its name from the so-called "grottoes" in Nero's *Domus Aurea* in Rome. Whilst by the end of the fifteenth century *grotesque* decorations began to appear in the paintings of artists such as Filippino Lippi, Pinturicchio and Signorelli, they were most fully developed in the second half of the sixteenth century, no accident considering how well the style adapted to the bizarre late-Mannerist taste of the age of Francesco I.
Amongst the subjects of the First Corridor are landscapes, real and fabulous animals, monsters, masks and satyrs, weapons and Medicean devices. In the frescoes of the vault illustrated here, situated half way down the First Corridor, we find various emblems of Francesco I de' Medici (the weasel with a branch of rue and the motto AMAT VICTORIA CURAM, "Victory loves care") and of Bianca Cappello, his lover and later his second wife (the oyster opening in the sun and the motto MAR [I] COELOQUE PROCREATA MERITO CARISSIMA, "Deservedly precious, she came forth from the sky and the sea").

Room 2 ◆ Giotto and the 13th Century

Rooms 2 to 9 are dedicated to medieval art, the early Renaissance, and the art of Pollaiolo. Room 8 is an exception, having been restructured in 1997 together with Room 15. The re-ordering of the rooms was carried out during the Fifties (architects Gardella, Michelucci and Scarpa, director Salvini). The wide opening in the entering wall allowed for the entry of large-scale works (Cimabue's Crucifixion *was previously hung here, and later returned to Santa Croce where it was damaged by the 1966 flood).*
Alongside some of the earliest examples of Tuscan painting, this first room with its truss-framed ceiling reminiscent of a medieval church houses three imposing Maestas *by Cimabue, Duccio and Giotto. Their recent restorations have provided new, important readings and confirm the great skill of Florentine carpenters in carrying out the complex carpentry of these three huge panels.*

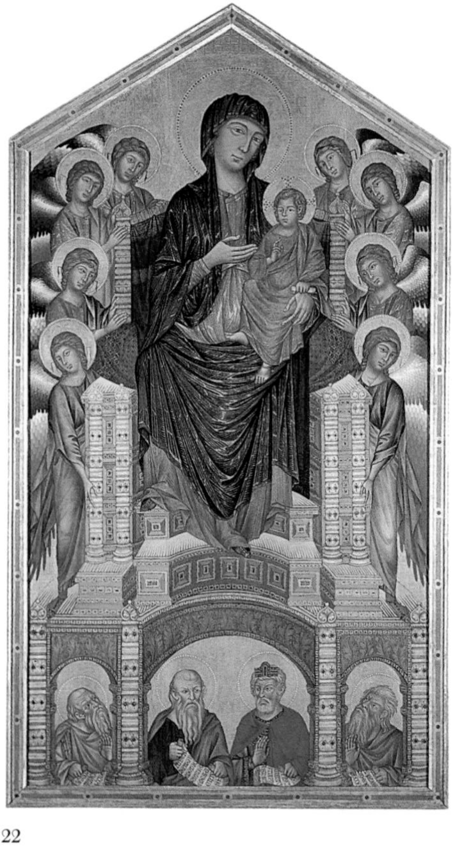

Cimabue

Maestà of Santa Trinita

Datable between 1280 and 1290
Tempera on wood, 425×243
Inv. no. 8343
In the Uffizi since 1919
Restored: 1993

This large panel painting, whose original frame is lost, was meant to stand 465 centimetres high on the main altar of the church of Santa Trinita, striking the view of all the faithful at once. Eight foreshortened angels flank the Madonna with Child. Below, between the arches, Jeremiah and Isaiah look upwards to confirm the prophecies inscribed on the scrolls, concerning the virginal birth of Jesus; in the middle are Abraham and David, from whose offspring the Saviour would rise.

DUCCIO DI BONINSEGNA
Maestà

c. 1285

Tempera on wood
450×293
Inv. unnumbered
In the Uffizi since 1948
Restored: 1989

Painted by Duccio for the Laudesi Confraternity Chapel in Santa Maria Novella, this is the first known large work of the Sienese painter. The outstanding frame, integrated into the altarpiece, surrounds the Madonna enthroned between six kneeling angels with thirty medallions showing saints and half-length Biblical figures, portrayed with intensity despite the small dimensions.

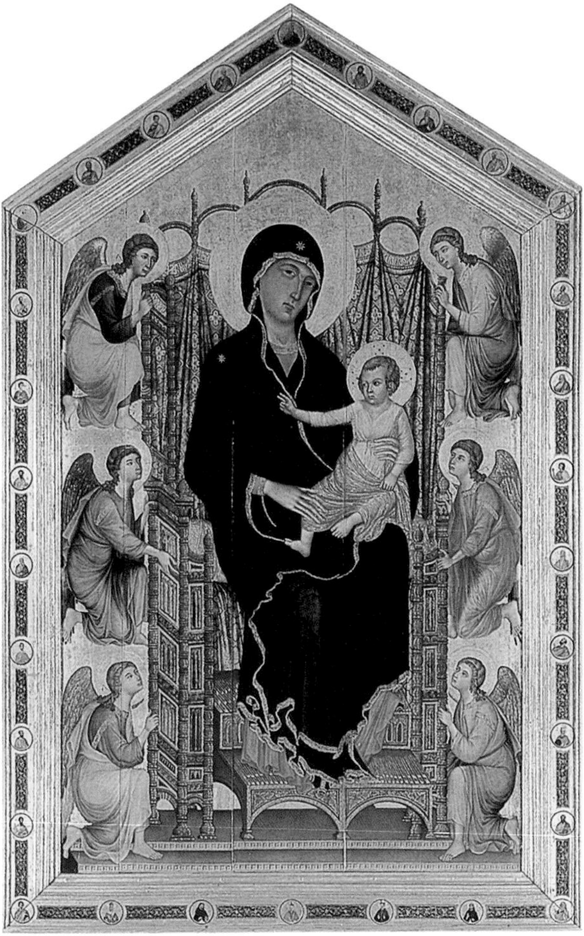

GIOTTO
The Ognissanti Madonna
(whole and details)
c. 1310
Tempera on wood
325×204
Inv. no. 8344
In the Uffizi since 1919
Restored: 1991

Painted for the Umiliati Altar, as recently proven, to the right hand side of the door of the screen wall in the church of Ognissanti, the gaze of the Madonna and the position of the throne in fact suggest it should be viewed from the right side, as with Duccio's *Maestà* in Santa Maria Novella. This large, devotional work is a homage to the virginity, maternity, and royalty of Mary. An angel offers her a precious crown, while another is giving the Child the eucharistic pyx, representing the Passion of Christ. Two angels at the Virgin's feet offer an ampulla with roses and lilies, both Marian symbols. Note the extraordinary perspective effect, with the figures solidly arranged in a space rendered lifelike by the three-dimensional throne. Note also the realism of the faces, of the variegated marble, of the flowers painted from nature and even of the wood of the platform at the feet of the Madonna.

Formerly on the main altar of the Badia Fiorentina, this panel painting shows the Madonna with Child, flanked on the left by St John the Evangelist and St Nicholas and on the right by St Peter and St Benedict.
On each pinnacle stands a small tondo (God the Father in the middle and angels on each side). Because of its articulated, architectural structure with pointed divisions and trefoil frames from which the saints appear to lean out, and because of its sensitive use of chiaroscuro and fine detail, the poliptych is considered to be the work of Giotto, completed after his travels to Rome and Rimini, and before his residence in Padua.

GIOTTO
Badia Poliptych
(whole and detail)

1295-1300

Tempera on wood
142×337
Inv. Dep. Santa Croce no. 7
In the Uffizi since 1957
Restored: 2009

SIMONE MARTINI AND LIPPO MEMMI
Annunciation

Signed and dated 1333

Below on the frame: "Symon Martini et Lippus Memmi de Senis me pinxerunt anno domini MCCCXXXIII"

Tempera on wood
184×210
Inv. nos. 451-453
In the Uffizi since 1799
Restored: 2001

This *Annunciation* was painted for the altar of Sant'Ansano in the Siena Cathedral and brought to the Uffizi by the Grand Duke Ferdinand III. The original frame is lost, but written beneath is an autograph documenting the date and the names of the painters, Simone Martini and his brother-in-law Lippo Memmi, who worked together in Siena in an extremely prolific workshop. On either side of the Annunciation are St Ansano and St Judith (or St Margaret). In the medallions above are the prophets Jeremiah, Ezechiel, Isaiah, and Daniel, carrying scrolls which represent the Incarnation (the central tondo, now lost, was to overhang the dove of the Holy Spirit and represent God the Father). Typically Sienese in its fine use of gold and its linearity accentuated by the sinuous, timid withdrawal of the Virgin, the work also contains precious realistic detail such as the variegated marble paving, the chequered cloak of the angel, the sumptuous vase of lilies, and finally the foreshortened, half-open book. The writing across the painting produces an almost theatrical effect, indicating the greeting by the angel to the Virgin.

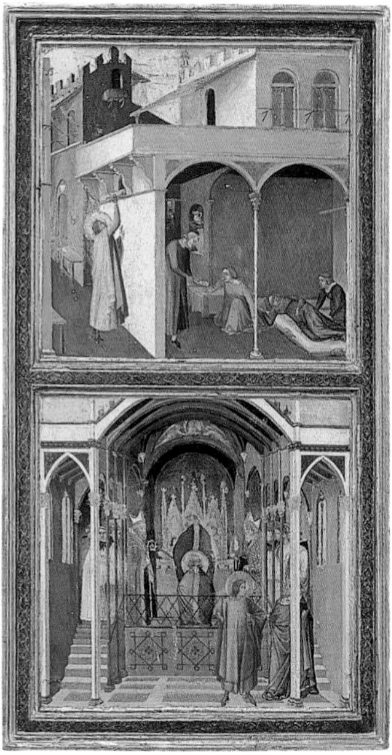

AMBROGIO LORENZETTI
Four Stories from the Life of St Nicholas
(Miracle of the possessed child, of the grain, of the poor youth; St Nicholas consecrated as Bishop of Myra)

c. 1330-1332
Tempera on wood
96×35 each panel
Inv. nos. 8348, 8349
In the Uffizi since 1919

In the church of San Procolo in Florence, Lorenzetti completed a panel painting (this was perhaps the *Triptych* with the *Madonna and Child, St Nicholas and St Proculous*, also in this room, inv. nos. 9411, 8731-8732). He also painted "stories of St Nicholas in small figures" in one of the church's chapels, a work which "enormously increased his name and reputation" (Vasari 1568).
On the two panels with stories of St Nicholas of Bari, part of a lost dossal or tabernacle, the Sienese painter proves himself not only a detailed story-teller, which would have been a striking quality for Florentines used to the simplicity of the Giottoesque narrative style, but also an artist attentive to problems of space.
A surprising vertical "fishbone" perspective is seen in the picture of the saint freeing the city of Myra from famine: in this innovative marine landscape, the eye of the viewer is lifted up to the open sails along the horizon; note also the devices of portraying the saint from behind, and of the showing the clerks emerging from behind columns in the scene of the Bishop's consecration.

AMBROGIO LORENZETTI
Presentation of the Virgin in the Temple

Signed and dated on frame 1342: "Ambrosius Laurentii de Senis fecit hos opus anno domini MCCCXLII"
Tempera on wood, 257×168
Inv. no. 8346
In the Uffizi since 1913
Restored: 1986

Painted for the altar of San Crescenzio in Siena Cathedral. The scene, with its complex setting which plays around the perspective lines of the paving, is much more attractive than the usual static figures of saints characteristic of altarpieces of the time. Its minute detail and the many descriptive and symbolic inscriptions invite our curiosity. The use of lacquer and costly lapis lazuli for the blue tones confirms the importance of the work, which was copied up until a century later by Sienese painters.

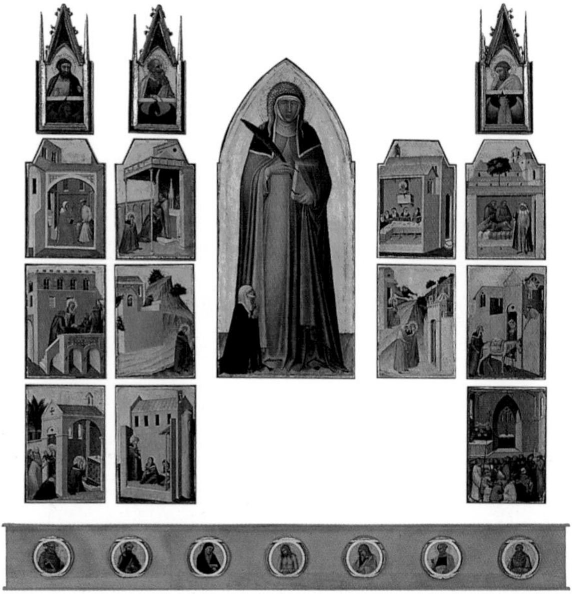

PIETRO LORENZETTI
Altarpiece of the Blessed Humility
(whole and detail)
c. 1340
Tempera on wood
51×21 (each pinnacle)
128×57 (central)
45×32 (each panel)
diam. 18 (tondoes)
Inv. nos. 8347, 6120-6126, 6129-6131
In the Uffizi since 1919

Painted for the altar of the Blessed Humility in the church of Saint John Evangelist in Florence, dismantled into various parts (located in Berlin and elsewhere), the painting was reassembled in 1954 on the basis of an eighteenth-century drawing. A benchmark of the mature work of Pietro Lorenzetti, here influenced by the quintessential solidity of the school of Giotto, the work represents eleven charming scenes from the miraculous life of the Blessed Humility, as she professes her humility (formerly known as Rosanese dei Negusanti, she was founder of the Vallombrosan convent of San Giovanni delle Donne di Faenza; she died in 1310).
At her feet, in the central panel, is perhaps St Margaret, second abbess of the monastery, who died in 1330 (this work was probably commissioned by her and painted after her death). On the three surviving pinnacles are the evangelists Mark, John, and Luke; on the predella is a *pieta* of Christ with the Virgin, and five saints within tondoes.

MASTER OF SANTA CECILIA
St Cecilia and Stories of Her Life
(whole and detail)

After 1304

Tempera on wood
85×181
Inv. no. 449
In the Uffizi since 1844

The fire which destroyed the church of Santa Cecilia in 1304 was recorded by the fourteenth-century chronicler Giovanni Villani; the church was rebuilt immediately afterwards and there is a convincing school of thought which holds that this altarpiece, among the most remarkable examples of the early 14th century Florentine school, was painted for this church just after the fire. It portrays Saint Cecilia enthroned, flanked by eight stories of her life, ending with her martyrdom. The scenes, characterised by a minutely detailed realism, echo Giotto's frescoes in the upper church at Assisi.
In this early evocation of the experiments of the young Giotto, however, the three-dimensional effect is still clearly in an experimental phase (note for example, top left, the carefully-prepared table for the wedding banquet of Cecilia and Valerian). Other works have also been attributed to this contemporary of Giotto, this master whose name comes from the altarpiece in the Uffizi: scenes from the life of Saint Francis in the frescoes of the lower church in Assisi and several oil panel paintings from the churches of San Giorgio alla Costa, San Simone and Santa Margherita a Montici in Florence.

BERNARDO DADDI
Poliptych of San Pancrazio

c. 1340
Tempera on wood
165×85 (central)
127×42 (sides)
31×17 (pinnacles)
diam. 20 (tondoes)
43×32 (predellas)
Inv. nos. 8458, 6127-6128, 8345
In the Uffizi since 1919

In 1568 Vasari attributed this poliptych, formerly on the main altar of the church of San Pancrazio, to another member of the Florentine school, Agnolo Gaddi. The central panel of the poliptych shows the traditional Madonna and Child enthroned with angels; to the sides are six panels with full-figure saints; above are fourteen small pinnacled panels with prophets and half-length portraits of saints and four tondoes with angels. On the predella are seven small panels with stories of the Virgin.
According to a likely reconstruction, at least six other pieces are missing and possibly also another predella, mentioned by Vasari, with stories of St Reparata, the Florentine patroness. This is therefore one of the most spectacular poliptychs of its time, although Vasari preferred only the smaller parts: "the only part of it which is really good, is the predella, filled with small figures".
Bernardo Daddi, amongst the most delightful of those representatives of the Giotto school who displayed miniaturistic tendencies, was in fact most at ease when narrating intimate, everyday scenes, peopled by graceful and lively figures.

GIOTTINO
Pietà
(whole and detail)

c. 1360-1365

Tempera on wood
195×134
Inv. no. 454
In the Uffizi since 1851

This panel painting, originally in the church of San Remigio, is considered one of the masterpieces of Florentine painting from the second half of the 14th century, for the rare psychological insight of the faces and for its luminous pictorial quality.
Along with the traditional characters mourning at the Deposition of Christ are two female figures dressed in contemporary 14th century clothing. One of them is a Benedectine nun, the other is a young, sumptuously dressed woman; both kneel to participate in the sorrowful event, protected by the hands of the patron saints Benedict and Remigius.
The artist, whose critical reputation is still hotly debated, was praised by Vasari for his "gentleness and sweetness", his ability to vary facial expressions and emotions, and to display the highest imaginative qualities through his brushwork.

ANDREA DI CIONE, KNOWN AS ORCAGNA AND JACOPO DI CIONE
St Matthew Triptych

c. 1367-1368
Tempera on wood
291×265
Inv. no. 3163
In the Uffizi since 1899
Restored: 1981

In 1367 the Bankers Guild commissioned Orcagna to paint a panel for the west pillar of its property in Orsanmichele, the seat of the Florentine Guilds. Considered to be among the best painters of his time and already a consultant for the works at the Cathedral, the artist became ill and the painting was completed by his brother Jacopo di Cione the following year. The unusual trapezoidal structure of the panel was created specifically for the pillar on which it was to hang. The central figure of St Matthew is flanked by four small scenes (Miracle of the Dragons, Calling of the Saint, Resurrection of King Egippus' son, Martyrdom of the Saint). Each scene is given an inscription. Above, the tondoes show the golden coins which symbolise the Bankers Guild. A work of great subtlety, it is enriched by details such as the rich brocade at the feet of the saint.

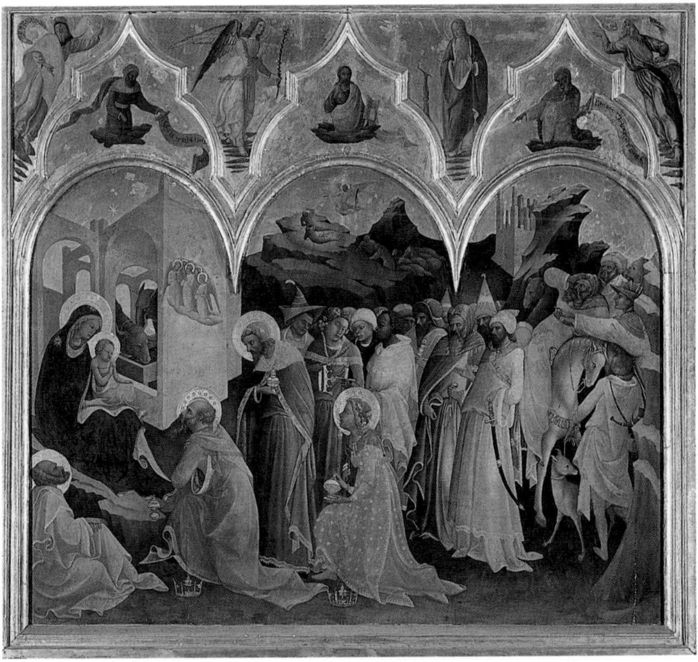

Lorenzo Monaco and Cosimo Rosselli
Adoration of the Magi

c. 1420-1422

Tempera on wood, 115×166
Inv. no. 466
In the Academy since 1810, in the Uffizi since 1844
Restored: 1995

The provenance of this panel painting is uncertain, but it is probably the altarpiece painted for the church of Sant'Egidio by Don Lorenzo, a Camaldolese monk from Santa Maria degli Angeli. It is also probable that the occasion for this was the reconsecration of the church by Pope Martin V. There may well have been a predella, now lost, such as in the contemporary *Adoration of the Magi* painted by Gentile da Fabriano (see catalogue below). Lorenzo Monaco, also a fine miniaturist, represented the liveliest and most up-to-date style of the age, and was the founder of a stylistic reformation which, starting from the experiences of the Giotto school, created lively figures displaying movement in every part of the body. Exotic devices stand out from the painting, such as the inscriptions in pseudo-Kufic (ancient Arabic) characters on the cloak of the standing Magus and the nearby figure between the three pinnacles depicting Christ bestowing blessings and two prophets, Cosimo Rosselli added two more prophets and the two figures of the Annunciation, transforming the tricuspid altarpiece into a rectangular one, more consonant with Renaissance style. The great altarpiece by Lorenzo Monaco showing the *Coronation* returned to this room after a long restoration.

GENTILE DA FABRIANO
Adoration of the Magi
(whole and detail)

Signed and dated 1423
Right partition not from the original predella
Tempera on wood
halo and friezes stamped with iron
300×283 (total)
173×220 (panel)
Inv. no. 8364
In the Uffizi since 1919
(Right predella panel in the Louvre since 1812)
Restored: 2004

Palla Strozzi, a man of learning and great wealth, a rival of the Medici who was once exiled to Padua, commissioned this sumptuous work for his family chapel in the church of Santa Trinita, where he planned the building of a public library with Greek and Latin volumes. His humanist education with Byzantine influences is reflected in this work by Gentile da Fabriano, who, originally from the Marches, was by 1420 living in Florence as a tenant of Palla Strozzi.

With its rich use of gold, applied to the panel in relief at certain points, the painting was to represent publicly the affluence and culture of the client, and to echo the words of Leonardo Bruni, Chancellor of the Republic: "The possession of external wealth affords the occasion to exercise virtue". The Adoration in the centre of the panel is simply the culminating moment of the fabulous procession of the Magi, which winds its way down from the top of the

panel, beneath a night sky illuminated by the star of Bethlehem. The eye is drawn to many details: from the numerous flowers, all drawn from nature, to the small pillars, to the fabrics woven with gold, and the harnesses of the horses. This analytical intensity of detail would seem to correspond to the literary style typical of Greek humanism, the so-called *ekphrasis*, which allows the minute, elaborate description of multiple elements.

MASACCIO E MASOLINO
Saint Anne Metterza
(whole and detail)
c. 1424
Tempera on wood
175×103
Inv. no. 8386
In the Uffizi since 1919

This work, formerly in the church of Sant'Ambrogio, was fundamental to the evolution of early Renaissance painting, and was the fruit of a collaboration between Masolino and his younger countryman Masaccio (they later worked together on the Brancacci Chapel in the Carmine church). St Anne and the angels are generally attributed to Masolino, with the exception of that on the top

right of the painting, probably done by Masaccio, who was also responsible for the Virgin with Child. The symbolic meaning of this altarpiece is, despite the simplicity of its composition, quite complex. It is not known under what circumstances the work was commissioned. The three main figures, St Anne, the Virgin, and the Child, placed along the same axis, have the static quality of Byzantine Madonnas (but the plasticity of the figures is entirely 15th century, and the angel swinging the censer introduces a sense of movement).

According to new theories, the panel may have been placed within a great devotional ciborium in the church of Sant'Ambrogio. In similar vein to the later *Coronation* by Filippo Lippi, originally situated in the same church and now in the Uffizi (Room 8), this work, inspired by the cults of Corpus Domini and the Immaculate Conception venerated in Sant'Ambrogio, represents the concept of a benevolent authority exercised by the Church within Christian society. The title of the work, "Saint Anne Metterza" (from the medieval Latin "met", the same, and "tertius", the third), is normally used in art history to refer to representations of the mother of the Virgin with her daughter and the Child sitting between her knees. In this painting St Anne acquires a key symbolic value, and probably also alludes to the historical figure of the abbess of the convent. To the faithful she represents a mother who protects a daughter who is without sin and who is the progenitress of the body of Christ. It is no mere fancy that the scholar Roberto Longhi should have recognised the silhouette of Brunelleschi's cupola in the open arms of the saint, as they lean upon Mary's shoulders in a gesture of protection. For the cupola itself, "climbing steeply to the skies", "wide enough to cover the whole of the Tuscan people with its shadow", as the great architect Leon Battista Alberti wrote in the 15th century, clasps the city of Florence in an ideal embrace.

Paolo Uccello
The Battle of San Romano

Signed on the hield at lower left: PAVLI VGIELI OPVS

c. 1438

Tempera on wood
182×323
Inv. no. 479
In the Uffizi since the second half of the 18th century
In restoration (2010)

Along with two panels in London and Paris, that of the Uffizi forms part of a cycle portraying different stages of the Battle of San Romano, where in Valdelsa the Florentines defeated the Duke of Milan, ally of the Sienese and the Emperor in 1432.

In 1492 an inventory of the belongings of Lorenzo the Magnificent listed this painting as existing in Palazzo Medici, and this was thought to be its original provenance, having been commissioned by Cosimo de' Medici the Elder.
An important discovery

by Francesco Caglioti has now put an end to a discordant whirl of hypotheses on the dating of the cycle.
Its intriguing history, only briefly outlined here, has been traced on the basis of incontrovertible archival data. The series was painted for a certain Bartolini, perhaps Lionardo, a leading figure in Florentine politics, who refurnished his home in Porta Rossa around 1438.
After some decades the three panels, transferred to the family residence at Santa Maria a Quinto by the heirs, were forcefully acquired by Lorenzo the Magnificent from the brothers Andrea and Damiano Bartolini.
The latter, after a "long and never resolved dispute", managed to get them back again in 1495.

BEATO ANGELICO
Coronation of the Virgin

c. 1435
Tempera on wood
112×114
Inv. no. 1612
In the Uffizi since 1948

At the beginning of the 16th century, a description by the Anonimo Gaddiano places this panel by Giovanni da Fiesole, otherwise known as Fra Angelico, in the church of Sant'Egidio in the Hospital of Santa Maria Nuova, "where Paradise is painted". It had been mentioned before by the biographer Antonio Manetti and identified by Vasari as being on the screen wall of the same church. Fra Angelico painted another *Coronation* with a different composition (now in the Louvre) possibly just before this, for the church of the convent of San Domenico below Fiesole, where he lived for a long time.
The work in the Uffizi, which probably formed a whole with two predellas now in the Museum of San Marco (*Wedding* and *Funeral of the Virgin*), is intensely illuminated by a profusion of gold and clever use of light; its perspective is created by a series of small clouds which drift into the background. Surrounding the *Coronation*, emphasised by the "firework" effect of a burst of golden rays, is a great circle of saints and angels (note the impact of the trumpets crossing over each other).

Domenico Veneziano
Santa Lucia dei Magnoli Altarpiece

c. 1445
Signed on the step of the throne
Tempera on wood
209×216
Inv. no. 884
In the Uffizi since 1862

Formerly in the church of Santa Lucia dei Magnoli, the altarpiece is today without its extraordinary predella, which has been dismantled and divided amongst the museums of Washington, Cambridge and Berlin. Its innovative use of light makes it one of the masterpieces of its time. Instead of the traditional medieval triptych, the sacred conversation takes place within a harmonious architectural structure of three arches with inlaid marble on the façade, rendered still more delicate by the pastel tones of rose and green, and enriched by a multicoloured pavement in receding squares. The morning light is emphasised by the shadow falling on the Virgin and Child. The branches of a citrus orchard stand out against an intensely realistic sky. In the foreground are St Francis, St John the Baptist, St Zanobius (patron of Florence, wearing rich costume with fabric and jewels of the era) and St Lucia, to whom the church was dedicated.

The Venetian painter, with whom the young Piero della Francesca had collaborated on the church of Sant'Egidio, died in poverty in Florence, his chosen city.

FILIPPO LIPPI
The Novitiate Altarpiece

c. 1445

Tempera on wood
196×196
Predella of the Pesellino with stories of saints, not illustrated, and divided between the Louvre and the Uffizi (two of the five stories are copies, inv. no. 8355)
Inv. no. 8354
In the Uffizi since 1919
Restored: 2010

In 1445 Michelozzo, architect of Cosimo the Elder, completed the Novitiate Chapel in the Franciscan church of Santa Croce. For ornamenting the altar, Cosimo called on Filippo Lippi whose patron he was (he may have written this apology for the transgressive friar/painter: "Great minds are heavenly forms and not dray horses for hire"). The architectural background of the altarpiece has a classical structure, in tune with Michelozzo's taste. The red Medicean emblems on the top of the frieze and the marble of the pavement enliven the composition with chromatic highlights, in an almost Flemish manner. It represents the Madonna enthroned with Child and saints, also seated: from left to right, Francis (patron of Santa Croce), Cosmas and Damian (Medici patron saints), and Anthony of Padua.

Filippo Lippi
Madonna with Child and Two Angels

c. 1465

Tempera on wood
95×63.5
Inv. no. 1598
In the Uffizi since 1796
Restored: 2005

This painting is today among the most admired in the Gallery. The Madonna, her hair entwined with precious pearls, has an enchanting profile, believed to be that of Lucrezia Buti, a nun with whom the friar/painter was scandalously in love. The sacred group, which also inspired Botticelli, Lippi's assistant in Prato, stands out from its frame with a delicacy similar to the classical-style reliefs of Donatello and Luca della Robbia (the pose of the angel in the foreground is probably derived from a putto on a classical sarcophagus). The background, a magnificent painting-within-a-painting, seems to anticipate the expansive landscapes of Leonardo.

FILIPPO LIPPI AND ASSISTANCE
Coronation of the Virgin
To the right, two details:
Self-portrait and St Theophista with Sons

1439-1447
Signed by "Frater Filippus" below, centre, on the platform
Tempera on wood, 200×287
Two tondoes with the *Annunciation*, remounted at an unspecified time, diam. 21
Inv. no. 8352
In the Uffizi since 1919
Restored: 1978

This was previously in Sant'Ambrogio, on the main altar which was restored by the prior Francesco Maringhi in 1441. Lippi's payments for the work began in 1439. Various painters collaborated in the prestigious undertaking: Piero di Lorenzo, Bartolomeo di Giovanni, Corradini da Urbino, Fra Diamante, a young disciple of Lippi, and at least two able carpenters, Manno de' Cori and Domenico del Brilla. The original composition of the frame is lost and part of the predella is in a Berlin museum. In 1446 the altarpiece was transferred to the painter's home in the convent of Sant'Apollonia where the blue pigment used to finish the painting was available, and one year later the work was finally in Sant'Ambrogio. Considerable amazement must have been provoked by the crowded scene of the *Coronation of the Virgin*,

whose arrival in Heaven is perhaps suggested by the intense, diagonal strips in blue and azure. Among the characters, at the extreme left stands St Ambrose; kneeling below is the presumed self-portrait of the friar who looks out at the spectator with a bored air; in the centre is St Eustace with his two small sons and wife Theophista; to the right is the donor next to the inscription, "Is perfecit opus" (He finished the work).

Filippino Lippi
Madonna with Child and Saints

1486 (signed and dated February 20, 1485 according to the Florentine style)
Tempera on wood
355×255
Inv. no. 1568
In the Uffizi since 1782

Previously in the Council Hall of Palazzo Vecchio, 1.200 lire was paid for the altarpiece at the wish of Lorenzo de' Medici. Some artisans collaborated with Filippino Lippi on the frame and on the curtain which was to veil the panel on the altar. The saints who flank the Madonna enthroned and crowned by angels, confirm the civic importance of the painting: John the Baptist and Victor, patrons of Florence and of the Guelph party; Bernard, on whose book is the word "*medica*", perhaps an implicit reference to the Medici family; and Zanobius, patron of the diocese, wearing a jewel on his cloak displaying the red lily, a symbol of Florence.

FILIPPINO LIPPI AND ASSISTANCE
Adoration of the Magi

Signed and dated on the back 1496
Tempera with oil on wood
258×243
Frame lost and predella divided between the Raleigh Museum (North Carolina) and private collection
Inv. no. 1566
In the Uffizi since 1666
Restored: 1985

In 1496 Filippino Lippi painted this *Adoration* for the Augustinian convent of San Donato in Scopeto (demolished 1529), to replace one which was never finished by Leonardo (Uffizi, inv. no. 1594); he was probably helped by other artists as indicated by recent restoration. Among the contemporary portraits included in the sacred event, situated in a landscape of classical ruins and castles, to the left are the Medici "Popolani": the old man kneeling with the astrolabe, which alludes to the "astronomer" Wise Kings, is Pierfrancesco di Lorenzo; behind him are his sons Lorenzo, Lord of Piombino, and Giovanni, who in 1496 was ambassador and married Caterina Sforza, by whom he was to have Lodovico, the future *condottiero* Giovanni dalle Bande Nere and father of Cosimo I. The three characters portrayed are from the Medici line which relinquished its power in fidelity to the Republic of Savonarola: here the crown is taken from Giovanni's head while his brother offers him a precious cup to present to the Child Jesus.

Piero della Francesca
Diptych of the Duke and Duchess of Urbino
Front panels with the portraits of Battista Sforza and Federigo II da Montefeltro

c. 1467-1472

Tempera on wood
47×33 each
Inv. nos. 3342, 1615
In the Uffizi since 1773
Restored: 1986

In the 15th century, as in antiquity, the diptych was considered a particularly precious work and was originally joined by a hinge, to be opened like a book or on occasion to be presented as a gift.
Painted on both sides (on the outer were the two *Triumphs* shown in the following pages), the famous diptych of Urbino, formerly in the Sala delle Udienze in the Ducal Palace, arrived in Florence in 1631 with the inheritance of Vittoria Della Rovere, wife of the Grand Duke Ferdinand II. It shows the Duke and Duchess of Urbino facing one another in solemn profile, in the classical medallion style which was very much in vogue during the humanistic period.

The precision of the features, focusing even on the less attractive details such as Federigo's nose, broken during a tournament, is a typical characteristic of Flemish art and confirms that Piero della Francesca (active in the court of Urbino) was one of the most sensitive interpreters of Nordic art, which was at that time well-known and popular from Ferrara to Florence and Urbino, right down to the south of Italy. Even the tidy landscape in the background, fading towards the distant hills and the horizon, possibly evoking the territory of Montefeltro, the Duke's land, is treated with an almost miniaturistic technique. Without using the traditional expedient of a curtain or window, the magnificent bird's-eye view unites the perspective of the two panels. The great painter from Sansepolcro was also in fact the author of important theoretical treatises on perspective, such as the *De Prospectiva pingendi*.

CLARVS INSIGNI VEHITVR TRIVMPHO ·
QVEM PAREM SVMMIS DVCIBVS PERHENNIS ·
FAMA VIRTVTVM CELEBRAT DECENTER ·
SCEPTRA TENENTEM

PIERO DELLA FRANCESCA
Diptych of the Duke and Duchess of Urbino
Rear panels with the *Triumphs* of Battista Sforza and Federigo II da Montefeltro

c. 1467-1472

Tempera on wood
47×33 each
Inv. nos. 1615, 3342
In the Uffizi since 1773
Restored: 1986

The two scenes of allegorical carriages, whose figurative meanings during this age of humanism were derived from the 14th century poetical *Triumphs* of Petrarch, serve to indicate the moral values of the two subjects. Each spouse is solemnly accompanied on the triumphal carriage by four Virtues: the theological Virtues for Battista Sforza (Faith, Charity, Hope, and Modesty) and the cardinal virtues for Federigo (Prudence, Temperance, Fortitude, and Justice). Battista, reading intently, rides a carriage pulled by two unicorns, a symbol of purity and chastity, the reins held by a small angel. The landscape in the background is probably that of Valdichiana. Standing behind Federi-

QVE MODVM REBVS TENVIT SECVNDIS ·
CONIVGIS MAGNI DECORATA RERVM ·
LAVDE GESTARVM VOLITAT PER ORA ·
CVNCTA VIRORVM ·

go, Victory, symbolised as an angel, is crowning him; the lake in the background can be identified as Lake Trasimeno.

Recent hypotheses suggest that two paintings on the reverse were painted on a subsequent occasion to the portraits on the front, that is to say after the death in childbirth of Battista Sforza, who in July 1472 gave birth to Guidubaldo, the long-awaited heir. That the Duchess was already dead when Piero della Francesca depicted her on the back of the panel would be confirmed by the tone of the Latin inscription inscribed on the classical-style marble beneath her image: "The name of the woman who knew how to be moderate during favourable times flies from mouth to mouth, adorning with praise the exploits of her great husband".

Under the triumphal carriage of her husband is a further inscription: "A man proclaimed worthy to hold the sceptre by the imperishable fame of his virtues, a renowned man equal to the most celebrated *condottieri*, is carried in great triumph".

ANTONIO AND PIERO DEL POLLAIOLO
St Jacob, St Vincent and St Eustace (Cardinal of Portugal's Altarpiece)

1466-1468

Oil on wood
172×179
Original frame, painted and gilded, attributed to Giuliano da Maiano (In the centre, in enamelled brass, Cardinal's coat of arms by the Pollaiolo brothers)
Inv. no. 1617
In the Uffizi since 1800
Restored: 1994

This painting was for the altar of the Cardinal of Portugal's Chapel in San Miniato al Monte. It has been replaced with a copy. The chapel, on which the major artists of that time worked, is dedicated to Jacob of Lusitania, Cardinal of Lisbon, who died in Florence in 1459, aged 25. The Pollaiolo brothers ran a prolific Florentine workshop dealing in painting, sculpture and goldsmithery. Their altarpiece, made of oak, has been given an unusual oily priming, typical of Flemish art. The work displays the fascination of the period for richly varied compositions: it is magnificent in its garments studded with jewels, the landscape which one glimpses beyond the balustrade, the variegated marble paving, and many other fine details.

The pilgrims' shell can be seen on the hat resting at the feet of St Jacob of Compostela, the patron saint of pilgrims.

Antonio Pollaiolo
Portrait of a Woman

c. 1475

Tempera on wood
55×34
Inv. no. 1491
In the Uffizi since 1861
Restored: 2008

The woman is portrayed in a half-bust profile on a rich background of blue lapis lazuli. Around her neck is a pearl necklace with a particularly beautiful pendent, which shows an angel in relief overlying a large ruby. She is wearing a head-dress typical of 15th century Florentine ladies: a veil covers her ears and the "honeycomb" plait in her golden hair is delicately highlighted by pearls.

ANTONIO POLLAIOLO
Hercules and Antaeus
Hercules and the Hydra

c. 1475
Oil tempera on wood
16×9 e 17×12
Inv. nos. 1478, 8268
In the Uffizi since 1789, dispersed during World War II, recovered in 1963, returned to the Uffizi in 1975
Restored: 1991

Around 1460 Pollaiolo painted three large canvasses of the *Labours of Hercules* for the Palazzo Medici. They were commissioned by Cosimo the Elder or perhaps his son, Piero (but not by the 11-year-old Lorenzo de' Medici, as some have claimed). The paintings may be part of a cycle on defeated tyranny (the character of Hercules, defender of order and justice and a legendary symbol of Florence, does in fact represent both political and religious virtues). The two panels from the Uffizi, with a third piece in a private collection on which Antonio's brother Piero collaborated, are most probably smaller copies, also by Pollaiolo, of the lost cycle.
The sculptural, dynamic tension of the bodies is typical of Antonio del Pollaiolo, who is famous for his studies of nude and anatomy.

SANDRO BOTTICELLI
Fortitude

1470

Tempera on wood
167×87
Inv. no. 1606
In the Uffizi since 1861
Restored: 1998

First datable work of Sandro Botticelli, *Fortitude*, along with a Virtue which was never executed, was commissioned from the artist in 1470 by the Florentine Merchants Guild to decorate the banisters in the Hall of Audiences in their palazzo, which was near that of the Signoria. Other six Virtues from the series (in this same room) had already been requested from Piero del Pollaiolo, which it appears he was late in delivering.

This room, created in 1943 from the upper part of the Medici Theatre (the beams are still visible), houses the foremost collection of Botticelli in the world. An initial layout was created in the postwar period with the altarpieces of Filippino Lippi, Perugino and Signorelli. In the 'fifties works by Botticelli began to be transferred here, and by 1978 the layout was more or less as we see it today, apart from one or two transfers at the beginning of the 'nineties (Filippino Lippi was relocated to Room 8). Botticelli's formation as an artist is displayed here through both sacred and profane works: from the early works which still show the influence of Filippo Lippi, Verrocchio and Pollaiolo, to those conceived in the intellectual circle of the Medici, to the mystic paintings of his mature years. Other cultural tendencies of the age are represented in this room by Ghirlandaio, an artist receptive to Flemish painting, which in turn is also represented here by the large poliptych of Van der Goes.

SANDRO BOTTICELLI

Portrait of a Young with a Medal

c. 1470-1475
Tempera on wood
and gilded gesso (medal)
56.5×44
Inv. no. 1488
In the Uffizi since 1666
Restored: 1991

Previously owned by Cardinal Carlo de' Medici. An enigmatic youth stares out at the spectator from a Flemish-style landscape. The medal, coined in 1464, showing the profile of Co simo the Elder *Pater Patriae* with the inscription MAGNUS COSMUS MEDICES PPP, supports the theory that the sitter was either linked to the Medici circle or was Antonio Filipepi, goldsmith and medallist, and brother of the artist.

Sandro Botticelli
The Return of Judith

The Discovery of the Body of Holofernes

c. 1470-1472
Tempera on wood
31×24 and 31×25
Inv. nos. 1484, 1487
In the Uffizi since 1632

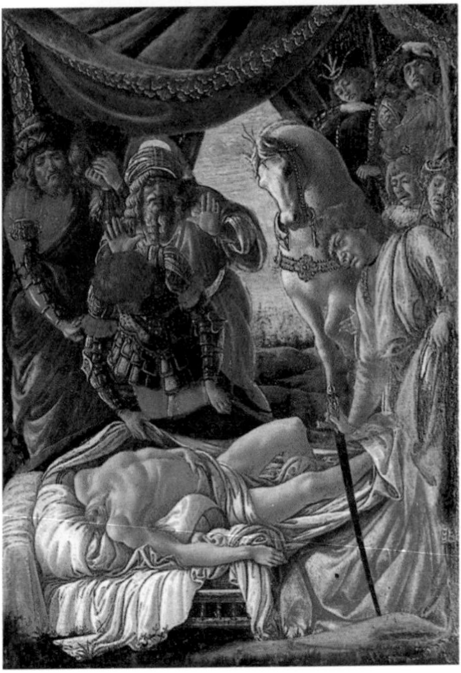

Originally part of a precious diptych with a carved and gilded walnut frame (now lost), the panels were documented in 1584 as a gift from the collector Ridolfo Sirigatti to the Grand Duchess Bianca Cappello, second wife of Francesco I; they were then passed down to her son, Don Antonio, who lived in the Casino in Via Larga from 1588. Judith, a biblical heroin, is the model of feminine virtue and of justice bringing victory to the weak. The diptych comes from Botticelli's early years, and perhaps shows the influence of Pollaiolo in the perfect integration of figure and landscape. The artist was however clearly original in his knowledgeable combinations of colours and in the use of light to illuminate clothing as well as the bedsheet on which the decapitated corpse of Holofernes sprawls, a splendid nude study.

SANDRO BOTTICELLI
Sant'Ambrogio Altarpiece (or of the *Converted Sisters*)
c. 1467-1470
Tempera on wood
170×194
Inv. no. 8657
In the Uffizi since 1946
Restored: 1992

This work was transferred to the Gallery of the Accademia in 1808 from the Benedictine monastery of Sant'Ambrogio, and it was originally thought that the work had been there since its completion. However, neither Sant'Ambrogio nor any of the Benedictine patron saints are portrayed, but instead Cosmas and Damian, saints traditionally linked with the Medici, who kneel at the feet of the Madonna; also are Mary Magdalen, John the Baptist, St Francis and St Catherine of Alexandria. The presence of St Francis of Assisi suggests that this might be the Botticelli panel seen by Vasari in the church of St Francis in Montevarchi, but this hypotheses has yet to be confirmed.
However, the theory that the altarpiece originated in the convent of the Converted Sisters, which for a long time gave its name to the painting, has now been refuted.
Now that many layers of overpainting have been removed by delicate restoration, the original style of the work has re-emerged, to make it a definite attribution and the first known altarpiece by this artist.
The composition and the pictorial *ductus* now show clear evidence of the influence of Filippo Lippi, whose pupil Botticelli was until the monk left for Spoleto in 1467. The influence of Verrocchio can also be seen in the almost metallic quality of the garments; he became Sandro Botticelli's master in that same year.

SANDRO BOTTICELLI
Adoration of the Magi
(whole and detail)

c. 1475

Tempera on wood
111×134
Inv. no. 882
In the Uffizi since 1796
Restored: 1980

Painted for the chapel of Guasparre Lami (agent of the Bankers Guild whose members included the Medici), in the church of Santa Maria Novella, this altarpiece is a public homage to Lorenzo the Magnificent and his family, with whom Botticelli was in contact. Against a backdrop of ancient ruins a favourite scene of the Medici is shown – the procession through the streets in which they took part every year with the Confraternity of Magi, dressed as oriental kings. Apart from the self-portrait of Botticelli which stares at the viewer from the right of the painting, Giuliano de' Medici stands out on the left; leaning on him is the poet Poliziano with Pico della Mirandola beside him. The Magus kneeling at the feet of Jesus is Cosimo the Elder, whilst the king with the red cloak seen from behind is Piero the Gouty, the father of Lorenzo (seen in profile on the right, with a short black garment).

DOMENICO GHIRLANDAIO
Madonna Enthroned with Angels and Saints

c. 1480
Tempera on wood
191×200
Inv. no. 881
In the Uffizi since 1853
Restored: 1981

Originally on the altar of San Giusto degli Ingesuati, a church which was demolished in 1530 during the siege of Florence, the painting was transferred to San Giovanni Battista della Calza where it was seen by Vasari. Against the background of a crystal clear sky, a balustrade covered in jewels supports the enthroned Virgin, surrounded by four garlanded angels – a composition which had become well-established in Florence by this period. The Child is blessing San Giusto, the patron saint of the church, who kneels at the front of the painting. The other figures are archangels Michael and Raphael, standing, and St Zanobius, patron saint of Florence, kneeling on the right. Standing out against the landscape are cypresses, a hibiscus and an orange tree. Vasari praised the metallic brilliance of the Archangel Michael's armour, obtained not through the application of gold, but with pure colour, an innovation first attributable to this artist. Ghirlandaio, also a fine portraitist, was one of the main artists to take an interest in the novelties of Flemish art, the influences of which can be seen in his landscapes and his special attention to decorative detail.

Sandro Botticelli
Madonna of the Magnificat

c. 1481-1485

Tempera on wood
diam. 118
(frame not original)
Inv. no. 1609
In the Uffizi since 1785
Restored: 1981

This famous tondo, in which the figures appear as if reflected in a convex mirror, takes its title from the beginning of the Virgin's prayer which can be read in the open book. The Child is holding a pomegranate, whose ruby red pips symbolise the Passion of Christ. A few years later the same artist was to paint another tondo, known as the *Madonna of the Pomegranate*, for the Sala delle Udienze of the Massai di Camera in Palazzo Vecchio, which is also displayed in this room. Its rare and splendid frame, the original, carved with the golden lilies of Florence against a blue background as on the ceiling of the Sala delle Udienze, has recently been attributed to the workshop of Giuliano da Maiano.

Sandro Botticelli
Coronation of the Virgin (Altarpiece of San Marco)

c. 1488-1490

Tempera on wood
375×256
Inv. no. 8362
In the Uffizi since 1819
Restored: 1990

Commissioned in 1488 by the Goldsmiths Guild for the chapel of their patron Saint Eligio in San Marco. After a long restoration the great altarpiece is now considered a key work of Botticelli's mature period, one of the most important to be painted in Florence during these years. The composition is very new for its time, being clearly divided into two zones: in the upper part, against a burst of golden rays, is the *Coronation of the Virgin* surrounded by dancing angels; below are the saints John the Evangelist, Augustine and Jerome, whose writings allude to the scene above, and on the extreme right is St Eligio. A deep sense of spirituality emanates from the painting, prefiguring later, still more mystical works such as *Calumny*.
The predella, divided by small painted columns, announces the themes of the altarpiece; among the stories of the saints is that of Eligio, who was also patron saint of blacksmiths, tricking a demon by shoeing the detached leg of a horse.

Sandro Botticelli
Calumny
(whole and detail)
c. 1495
Tempera on wood
62×91
Inv. no. 1496
In the Uffizi since 1773

Painted for Antonio Segni, a Florentine banker who was a friend of Leonardo, the painting is a complex allegory inspired by the work which Apelles is said to have painted to refute the calumny spoken against him to King Ptolemy Filelfo by a rival. In it the victim of the calumny is dragged before King Midas who is flanked by Suspicion and Ignorance. To the left stands Truth, naked as per tradition, next to Repentance.

SANDRO BOTTICELLI
Primavera
(whole and details
on the following pages)
c. 1482

Oil tempera on wood
203×314
Inv. no. 8360
Permanently in the Uffizi
since 1919
Restored: 1982

This famous painting, whose meaning is still the subject of much discussion, was in 1498 in the Via Larga house of Lorenzo and Giovanni di Pier-

francesco de' Medici, the cousins of Lorenzo the Magnificent. Like *Pallas and the Centaur* (also in this room), the panel hung over the back of a day-bed or chest. By the mid-sixteenth century it hung instead in the Medici villa at Castello, where Vasari described it as "Venus as a symbol of spring, being adorned with flowers by the Graces".

The complex allegory seems to have been inspired by the classical texts of Ovid and Lucre-

tius, and by certain verses of Agnolo Poliziano (1475), friend of the Medici and of the artist, who describes a garden with the Three Graces garlanded with flowers and the springtime wind Zephyrus chasing after Flora. The winged genie on the right of the painting is indeed generally thought to be Zephyrus who chased and possessed the nymph Chloris, and then married her, giving her the ability to germinate flowers (here she has blooms falling from her mouth). Near to Chloris is the smiling figure clothed in flowers, fixed forever in the collective imagination, representing the transformation of Chloris into Flora, the Latin goddess of Spring; the woman in the centre is possibly Venus, and this is her garden. The three women on the left entwined in a dance, derived from ancient images of the Three Graces, may be the symbol of Liberality. Above is Cupid, the blindfolded god of love. Finally, the youth with a traveller's hat, sword and winged sandals is certainly Mercury, herald of Jove, who is perhaps here as an emblem of knowledge.
The interpretations of this work are multifold. The allegory of Spring, the season in which the invisible world of Form descends to mould and shape Matter, may perhaps be celebrating the marriage of the erudite Lorenzo Pierfrancesco de' Medici, friend of Botticelli, and Semiramide Appiani, a female relative of Simonetta Vespucci, famous for her beauty and for her presumed liaison with Giuliano de' Medici.
A more recent interpretation, however, sees the painting as a metaphorical celebration of the Liberal Arts, to be read in a nuptial key. Whatever the case, the work remains one of the highest expressions of the ideal return to the golden age of Florence at the time of Lorenzo the Magnificent. The most probable date of the painting is around 1482, when the artist returned home from Rome. A detail to note: the flowers in the meadow number almost two hundred botanical species copied from nature, many of which flower on the hills of Florence in the spring. Botticelli has, however, mixed reality and fantasy: wild oranges do not, for example, appear in nature at the same time as so many other flowers.

Sandro Botticelli
The Birth of Venus
(whole and details
on the following pages)
c. 1484

Tempera on linen canvas
172.5×278.5
Inv. no. 878
In the Uffizi since 1815
Restored: 1987

The painting, whose origins and patron are unknown, was by the mid-16th century to be found together with the *Primavera* in the villa at

Castello, the former property of Lorenzo di Pierfrancesco de' Medici, who died in 1503. The title which, unusually for that period, made the painting famous, comes from the last century, and is based on a faulty interpretation of the subject as *Venus Anadiomene* ("arising from the sea"), a subject which the painter Apelles made famous in antiquity. In fact, Botticelli, inspired by the writings of Homer and Virgil and perhaps once again by the verses of his friend

Poliziano, is narrating a different episode from the legend of the goddess: her arrival at the island of Kythera or perhaps Cyprus.
Against a seascape rendered with the utmost mastery, Venus stands naked on a huge shell, being pushed towards shore by the swell of the sea, helped by the breath of the winds Zephyrus and Aura who embrace softly whilst roses fall from the sky. She is welcomed by a girl wearing a silken cloak embroidered with daisies and other flowers: this is possibly the Hora of Spring or one of the Three Graces. Whilst the figures on the left may be taken from the famous *Tazza Farnese*, now in the Archaeological Museum

in Naples but then in the gem collection of Lorenzo the Magnificent, the pose of the main figure is inspired by the antique sculptural type, the *Chaste Venus*, well-known since medieval times. Like the *Primavera*, this famous work is representative of the most serene and graceful phase of Botticelli's art, linked to the neo-Platonic atmosphere of Lorenzo's age: once again we are shown the fusion of Spirit and Matter, the harmonious marriage of Idea and Nature. Instead of the brilliant and solid colours used for the *Primavera*, it is painted with a mixture of diluted yolk and light tempera which give it an appearance similar to that of a fresco.

Hugo van der Goes
The Portinari Triptych
(whole and detail)

c. 1477-1478

Oil on wood
253×304 (central panel)
253×141 (side panels)
Inv. nos. 3191-3193
In the Uffizi since 1900

The triptych was painted in Bruges for Tommaso Portinari, an agent of the Medici and councillor of the Duchy of Burgundy. Portinari was in Flanders from 1455 and in 1470 married Maria Maddalena Baroncelli, by whom he had ten children. In this great triptych the spouses are portrayed on the side panels, absorbed in prayer before the *Adoration of the shepherds*, with patron saints and the three eldest children, Maria, Antonio and Pigello (born in 1474, the year from which the probable date of the painting is calculated).

The work was sent to Florence by the owners in 1483, destined for the main altar of the church of Sant'Egidio, their favourite church. The great Flemish triptych made a significant impact on the artists working in Florence during those years, particularly because of its minute attention to natural detail, so far removed from the simplicity of Florentine painting.

Room 15 ◆ Leonardo

This room was restructured and the display reorganised in 1991. The works, lit from above by a wide skylight, bear witness above all to the early phases of Leonardo's Florentine activity, from his beginnings in Verrocchio's studio to his departure for Milan in 1482. Also exhibited here are some recently restored panel paintings by the graceful Perugino, an Umbrian artist who was active in Florence at the end of the century, as well some works by the "eccentric" Piero di Cosimo, whose compositions were unusually inventive. The works of these two artists form an ideal link with other paintings carried out in Florence between the 15th and 16th centuries now on display in Room 19 (beyond the Tribune) and Room 25 (west wing).

Verrocchio and Leonardo da Vinci
Baptism of Christ
(whole and detail)

Variously dated c.1473-1478
Tempera and oil on wood
180×152
Inv. no. 8358
In the Uffizi since 1914
Restored: 1998

This newly restored panel painting came from the church of San Michele in San Salvi and confirms the vitality of Verrocchio's workshop which was amongst the most famous in Renaissance Florence. According to Vasari, Verrocchio gave up painting because his pupil Leonardo had surpassed him, but although Leonardo's hand has now been identified in the angel on the left and the background landscape, interventions by other artists are visible in this painting, which shows discrepancies of style and technique. The dry style of the palm tree and rocky outcrop behind John the Baptist's shoulders is very different from the mountains fading softly into the watery landscape beyond the heads of the angels. Christ and John the Baptist are also treated in different styles, the former smoothly finished, the latter harsher and more strained. Although no names have yet been put forward, it is clear that another important artist worked on this painting (the angel on the right has even been attributed by some to Botticelli), assisted, perhaps at different times, by apprentices.
Some details which were previously undetected are now visible, such as the fen birds in the far landscape and some fingerprints on the figure of Christ which indicates the direct application of fingertips to the paint. The final touches in oil on some parts of the painting are typical of Leonardo, whose participation in this work may not be as early in his career as has been thought until now, although this theory still needs verifying.

LEONARDO DA VINCI
Annunciation
(whole and detail)

Variously dated between c.1475 and 1480

Oil tempera on wood
98×217
Inv. no. 1618
In the Uffizi since 1867
Restored: 2000

New hypotheses for the reading of this painting have been stimulated by its restoration, completed in March 2000, which has revealed not only its luminosity and clarity of detail but a stronger sense of perspective in the architectural foreshortening on the right (the door, of which both doorjambs can now be seen, gives a clearer glimpse of the baldachin in the room).
Still controversial is the dating of the work painted in Florence for the Church of San Bartolomeo a Oliveto.
Hypotheses range from the early 1460s, when the artist was only a little over twenty, almost up to the beginning of the next decade. In some details the influence of Verrocchio, or perhaps Leonardo's homage to his master, can be recognized (especially in the base supporting the lectern, reminiscent of the Sepulcher of Giovanni and Piero de' Medici in San Lorenzo).
The Virgin's arm seems disproportionately elongated, unable to reach the book on the lectern, and the angel's shadow is too dark for the light of dawn, which restoration

has shown to be the hour chosen by Leonardo da Vinci as the setting, perhaps with symbolic overtones, for the Annunciation.
The meadow is sprinkled with a myriad of flowers studied from life; in the beautiful landscape, typical Tuscan cypresses trail off into the distance where the minute details of a lake-side city blend into the bluish tones of the bare rocky mountains in the background.

LEONARDO DA VINCI
Adoration of the Magi

1481

Mixed oil tempera on wood
243×246
Inv. no. 1594
In the Uffizi since 1670

This was transferred from the collection of Antonio and Giulio de' Medici to the Gallery in 1670 and later to Castello, to return to the Uffizi in 1794. The work was commissioned from Leonardo by the Augustinian monks of San Donato a Scopeto in 1481, but remained unfinished at the time of the artist's departure to Milan, one year later. To substitute it, several years later the monks asked Filippino Lippi to make a panel painting of a similar subject (Room 8). Because of the varnishes added during the centuries, the panel painting by Leonardo, which has remained in a monochrome state, is almost illegible. From recent research done on a preparatory drawing which once hung in the Gallery as a painting, a complex perspective system can be worked out. The magnificent setting is made up of several narrative episodes brought together by a kind of continuous motion; the scene filled with people and animals absorbs the spectator and was meant to give the illusion of a figurative metamorphosis from one group to another. The painting is rich in symbolic meanings; the ruins in the background allude, for instance, to the fall of paganism at the advent of Christ.

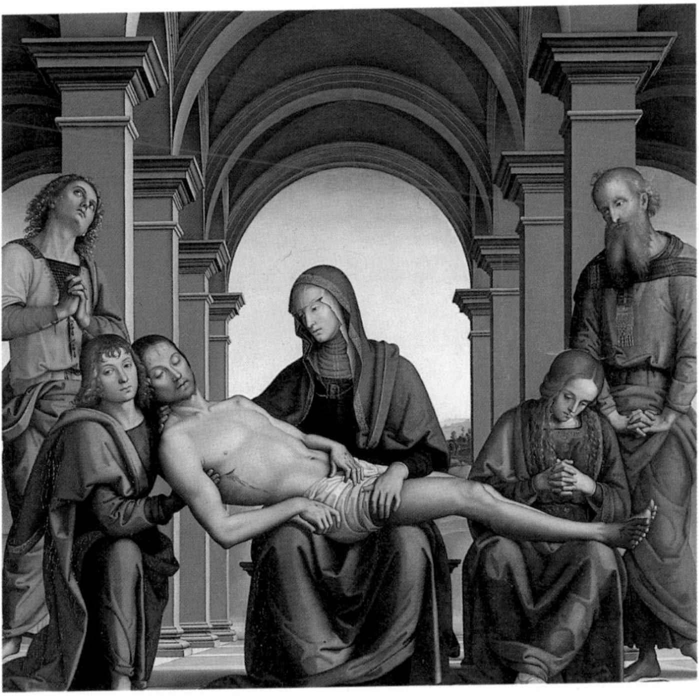

Pietro Perugino
Pietà

c. 1493-1494
Oil tempera on wood
168×176
Inv. no. 8365
In the Uffizi since 1919
Restored: 1984

This work, like the *Agony in the Garden*, also at the Uffizi, was painted by Perugino for the screen wall in the Ingesuati church outside the Pinti Gate. The panel painting (which once had a predella by Bartolomeo di Giovanni, now divided between other museums), underwent many transfers of location after the destruction of the convent in 1529. In an atmosphere of deep spirituality, perhaps already influenced by the sermons of Savonarola, the Madonna supports across her knees the rigid and ashen body of Christ. He is also supported by the kneeling John the Evangelist, who holds his face close to that of Christ, and by Mary Magdalen who is seated in prayer. Standing like statues, Nicodemus and Joseph of Arimathea serve as a link between the holy scene and the airy architectural structure.
The Umbrian artist was, from 1472, a member of the Painters Guild in Florence, and in those years he quickly became renowned in the Tuscan city, where he carried out many works including some preparatory cartoons for stained glass windows also in the convent of the Ingesuati, where there was a workshop producing glass and costly pigments.

PIETRO PERUGINO
Madonna and Child with Saints

Signed and dated 1493
Oil tempera on wood
178×164
Inv. no. 1435
In the Uffizi since 1784
Restored: 1995

This painting, carried out for the chapel of Cornelia Martini in the church of San Domenico di Fiesole, shows a Madonna enthroned between St John the Baptist and St Sebastian. The date is written on the scroll painted onto the base carved with classical motifs. This was the year when Perugino married the beautiful Chiara Fancelli, daughter of the architect Luca (who was also to work at the court of Mantua). Since its restoration, which has restored the correct balance of colours to the painting, the streaks down the right-hand pilaster behind St Sebastian are also more visible, and may evoke the idea of the column to which the saint was tied at his martyrdom according to tradition. The figure of the martyred saint was repeatedly portrayed by the painter, who, as Vasari says, often returned to those "same things" with which he had most success.

Piero di Cosimo
Incarnation of Christ

c. 1498-1505
Oil on wood; 206×172
Inv. no. 506
In the Uffizi since 1804
Restored: 1980

This was painted for the Tedaldi Chapel in the church of Santissima Annunziata (the predella is now lost). The pedestal has a relief showing the Annunciation, an episode prefiguring the moment when Christ became incarnate of the Virgin, through the dove of the Holy Spirit. Saints Catherine, John the Evangelist, Filippo Benizzi, Antonino, Peter, and Margaret attend the scene. At the highest point of the almost anthropomorphic landscape, typical of this imaginative artist, are the events which followed (the Adoration of Child, the Proclamation to the Shepherds, the Flight into Egypt). Above to the right is Monte Senario, home of the founders of the Order of the Servants of Mary. Recent studies which deny the traditional view of Piero as an "eccentric late-comer", have brought the date of the painting forward to before the end of the 15th century.

Room 16 ◆ Geographical Maps

At the time of Francesco I, this room was a terrace open towards the East, with two windows on another wall (later closed up) beside a fresco showing the island of Elba.

Around 1589 the new Grand Duke Ferdinand ordered a glass window to close the loggia, which was then frescoed by Ludovico Buti with geographical maps of Tuscany, following scientific surveys of the territory, drawn by the cartographer Stefano Bonsignori.

In the enthusiasm for scientific progress, which had already been shown by the Duke's father Cosimo for reasons which included political prestige, the room was set aside to house outstanding scientific instruments, such as the large wooden armillary sphere made by Antonio Santucci delle Pomarance (1593), the globe attributed to Ignazio Danti, and Galileo's telescope and astrolabe.

Still undergoing reorganisation, the room today includes some copies of these instruments which were transferred some time ago to the Museum of Science.

The ceiling is decorated with mythological canvases by Jacopo Zucchi, who painted them in Rome for Ferdinand de' Medici, who was then a Cardinal (c. 1572). They were later inserted between the beams which were decorated with garlands of fruit and flowers by Ludovico Buti.

Room 17 ◆ Hermaphrodite Room

This delightful little room, joined to the Tribune, dates back to the time of Ferdinand I, when it was called "The Mathematics Room". Today it takes the name of the Sleeping Hermaphrodite, *a sculpture from antiquity famous for its ambiguous sensuality, which has been on display here since 1669. The work, many variations of which exist in other museums, is a copy in Parian marble from the bronze original of Polykles and was acquired by Ferdinand II from the Ludovisi Collection in Rome.*
The inspiration for the room and its decorations came from Filippo Pigafetta, following his passion for geometry and mechanics. Around the year 1598, he suggested building a room devoted to "the study of military architecture", with a display of mechanical instruments, weight-lifting machines, "books, geographical maps and plans, and models of fortresses". Certain frescoes on the first ceiling (painted by Giulio Parigi, a painter, architect, and Medicean engineer), hint at the ambitions of the Grand Duke for expansion into foreign territories and nautical exploits. Others attest to the hydraulic skills of Tuscan technicians and the mathematical competence of his men-at-arms, with a celebration of the greatest historical figures in this field: Pythagorus, Ptolemy and Archimedes, this last portrayed during the siege of Syracuse.

ROOM 18 ◆ TRIBUNE

The octagonal Tribune was planned by Buontalenti in 1584, and with its cupola encrusted with mother-of-pearl shells set into a background of scarlet lacquer, it was for Francesco I the jewel in the Gallery's crown. Through windows made from Oriental crystal, natural light falls softly upon the paintings, on the walls covered in red velvet, on the sculptures and precious objects. The skirting board, now lost, painted by Jacopo Ligozzi, had a frieze with fish, birds, streams and plants. The room symbolises the cosmos and its elements: the lantern with its wind rose represents air; the shells, water; the red walls, fire; the marble and the semi-precious stones of the pavement, earth. In the centre, the octagonal jewel case (lost) encrusted with gold, gems, and rare stones, and with boxes decorated by Giambologna, echoed the shape of the room. Over the centuries the layout of the room has been rearranged many times, but the ancient sculptures are still here, pride of the Tribune since the 17th century, as is the table with its mosaic of semi-precious stones from the Opificio of the Grand Duke (1633-1649), and finally many paintings from 16th century Florence. The date 1601 recently found on the cupola indicates the year when the room was completed.

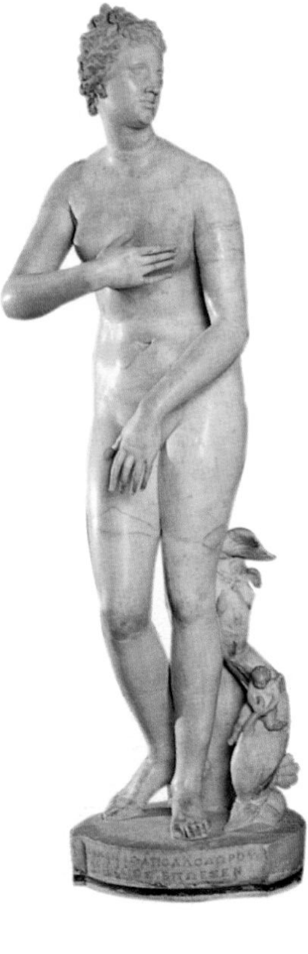

Medici Venus

Copy from an original
Greek of the 2nd
century BC.
Greek marble, h. 1.53 m
Inv. no. 224
In the Uffizi since 1677

The *Medici Venus*, one of the most celebrated classical sculptures of the granducal collection, was acquired at the beginning of the 17th century for the family's Roman villa on the Pincio in Rome, and was then transferred in 1677 from Villa Medici to the Uffizi by the Grand Duke Cosimo III. Despite the reputation of the Grand Duke as a bigot, this sculpture with its disturbing beauty (a type already known in Rome since at least the 12th century) took place of honour in the Tribune and soon became the focus of unrestrained admiration.

PONTORMO
Portrait of Cosimo the Elder

c. 1519-1520
Inscription on the scroll: uno avulso non deficit alter ("one broken branch does not weaken another")
Inscription behind the sitter's shoulders: COSM. MEDICES P.P.P. [Pater Patriae Parens]
Oil on wood, 86×65
Inv. no. 3574
In the Uffizi since 1914

This posthumous portrait of Cosimo the Elder (1389-1464) was commissioned by Goro Gheri, secretary of Lorenzo de' Medici, Duke of Urbino, most probably for the Medici Pope Leo X, at the suggestion of Ottaviano de' Medici. Portrayed in profile, as in a humanist medallion, the "*Pater Patriae*" has next to him the Medici emblem of a *broncone*, a broken branch with a new shoot hinting at the continuity of his descendants: the shoot is the future Duke Cosimo I, born from a cadet branch of the family in 1519, when after the Duke of Urbino's death the family lineage risked extinction. The painting, placed in the Tribune in 1638, was transferred to San Marco in 1869.

Rosso Fiorentino
Musical Cherub

Signed and dated 1521
Oil on wood
47×39
Inv. no. 1505
In the Tribune since 1605
Restored: 2000

This work was long believed to be a complete panel painting in itself, but recent research done with reflectography suggests that it is probably the fragment of an altarpiece with the Virgin and Saints, of which, however, there remains no other trace. The cherub probably sat on steps, indicated by parallel incisions on the surface of the painting. Down towards the right the signature (partially rubbed off) became legible, as did the date, perhaps painted by Rosso himself on the already separate fragment of the panel.
Only the much-needed restoration of this charming little cherub, so admired by visitors to the Tribune, will resolve any remaining doubts over stylistic questions. It is, however, possible that it was painted far from Florence, as the artist mentions his origin alongside his signature, declaring himself to be "florent [inus]". The development of this great artist, whose mode of expression was so unique in the art world of his time, often crossed over with that of artists who were strangers or "eccentrics", thanks his many journeys to other Italian cities, and his final destination at the Fontainebleau court of King François I in France.

ANDREA DEL SARTO
Woman with the 'Petrarchino'

c. 1528
Oil on wood
87×69
Inv. no. 783
In the Tribune since 1589
Restored: 1986

This young woman is smiling mysteriously, perhaps to her beloved, pointing in her book to the verses of two love sonnets by Petrarch: "Ite caldi sospiri al freddo core" ("Go, warm sighs, to the cold heart"; CLIII), and "Le stelle, il cielo et gli elementi a prova" ("The stars, the sky and the elements compete" CLIV). She is probably Maria del Berrettaio, born in 1513 from del Sarto's first marriage to his adored wife Lucrezia. The chosen subject of a woman with this book confirms the great reputation in the sixteenth century of this fourteenth century poet, whose book of rhymes (the so called 'Petrarchino') appears in many other portraits of the time.

BRONZINO
Lucrezia Panciatichi

c. 1541

Tempera on wood
102×83.2
Inv. no. 736
In the Uffizi since 1704
In the Tribune since 1763

Lying against Lucrezia's sumptuous dress, the gold and enamel plaques of her necklace carry the words, "AMOUR DURE SANS FIN", which attracted the fantasy of both Vernon Lee and Henry James. The book in her right hand is a Book of Daily Offices, with prayers dedicated to Mary. This intense portrait shows Lucrezia Pucci, wife of Bartolomeo Panciatichi, who was a Florentine academician from 1541. Panciatichi himself had his portrait done by Bronzino, who also painted a *Holy Family* for him (Room 27). Both the portraits, now in the Tribune, were in 1584 still to be found in the house of his son Carlo, a servant of Francesco I.

Bronzino
Eleonora di Toledo with her Son Giovanni

c. 1545
Oil on wood
115×96
Inv. no. 748
In the Uffizi since 1798

Eleonora di Toledo, wife of Cosimo I de' Medici from 1539, is shown here with her second son. Her highly-valued role as a mother is marked by the pomegranate on her clothing. This symbol of fertility is also present on the vault of her chapel in Palazzo Vecchio, also frescoed by Bronzino, prolific portraitist to the Medici court. The brocade dress with Spanish embroidery is identical to that found in 1857 inside the tomb of the Duchess in the Medici Chapel.
The background landscape may show the Grand Duke's dominions.

Cecchino Salviati
Charity

c. 1543-1545
Oil on wood
156×122
Inv. no. 2157
In the Uffizi since 1778
Restored: 2002

There are two *Charities* by Salviati recorded in Florence. This gifted master worked above all in Rome, where he was the godson of Cardinal Giovanni Salviati. It is unsure whether this allegory, with its rich sculptural references found in the Michelangelesque pose and the jewels adorning the figures, was the painting executed for the gem merchant Ridolfo Landi, or that documented in the Ufficio della Decima. Cecchino, who was much praised during his own time but who fell out of favour in the centuries which followed, is now being revalued as one of the most important members of the "*bella maniera*", which started with Michelangelo.

LORENZO DI CREDI
Annunciation

c. 1480-1485
Oil on wood
88×71
Inv. no. 1597
In the Uffizi since 1798

From the collection of Cardinal Leopoldo, this little masterpiece made by one of Verrocchio's pupils is a graceful composition, whose balance is helped by the false low-relief in the style of a predella, showing stories of Adam and Eve.

LUCA SIGNORELLI
Holy Family

c. 1484-1490
Oil on wood
diam. 124
Inv. no. 1605
In the Uffizi since 1802
Restored: 2000

Signorelli was born in Cortona and was active in Florence, Rome, and other Italian cities. Soon after this tondo, he painted another which was still more complex (inv. no. 502) and rich with classical references. This latter was probably commissioned by a member of the Medici family.

PIETRO PERUGINO
Francesco delle Opere

1494
Inscription on the scroll:
TIMETE DEUM (Fear God)
Oil on wood
52×44
Inv. no. 1700
In the Uffizi since 1833

This wonderful portrait is probably of Francesco delle Opere, as indicated on the rear of the painting. This Florentine artisan, who died in Venice in 1516, was the brother of a friend of the painter, Giovanni delle Corniole, a master gem cutter.
The 'photographic' precision of the features, the position of the figure with its hand leaning on the balustrade, and the landscape in the background, are clearly inspired by Flemish art, particularly by Memling's portraits which were already known in Florence (Room 22)

PIERO DI COSIMO
Perseus Liberating Andromeda

c. 1510-1513
Oil on wood
70×123
Inv. no. 1536
In the Tribune since 1589

Initially exhibited in the Tribune as a work in which Piero di Cosimo was following a drawing by Leonardo, this is now the artist's most famous painting precisely for its completely original composition. It narrates in great detail the myth of Perseus liberating Andromeda by killing the sea monster.
The central scene is dominated by the dragon in its death-throes, but the eye is also drawn to the fascinating, almost grotesque landscape, and to the detail in the painting – from the exotic turbaned figures at the far edges of the painting to the nordic wood and straw huts on the unlikely-looking hilltops in the background. The musical instruments are equally unlikely: they could never be played as they are all missing a sound box or strings. It has been suggested that the scene in this painting was inspired by the Florentine carnival of 1513 when the Medicis returned to the city – symbolised by the dried branch with its new shoot, the Medici *broncone* emblem.
A recent study suggests that the work, which according to Vasari was painted for one of the Strozzi family, belonged to Filippo the Younger, who in 1510 paid Piero for a "work" for his bedchamber.

As in the previous room and the four that follow, the original fresco decoration was carried out in 1588 by Ludovico Buti. The four views of Florentine spectacles on the vault were however repainted during the middle of the 19th century. Under the current layout, the room houses masterpieces from the great German painters, Dürer and Cranach, and the Flemish painter Bruegel the Elder. Amongst the works of Dürer (who made two key trips to Italy in 1494 and 1505), the Portrait of the Artist's Father *(1490) and the* Madonna with Pear *(1526) stand out, along with the* Adoration *discussed below.*

ALBRECHT DÜRER
Adoration of the Magi

Monogrammed
and dated 1504
Oil on wood
99×113,5
Inv. no. 1434
In the Uffizi since 1793
(side panels in Frankfurt, Colonie, Munich)
Restored: 2007

Painted just before Dürer's second trip to Italy, the intense colors and use of perspective are both reminiscent of Venetian painting, particularly that of Mantegna and Giovanni Bellini.
The classical ruins, typical of Italian painting, combine well with the nordic-style landscape with small figures in the distance. The careful study of plants and animals, so rich in symbolism, confirms Dürer's practise of studying nature, characteristic of most of this German master's work.

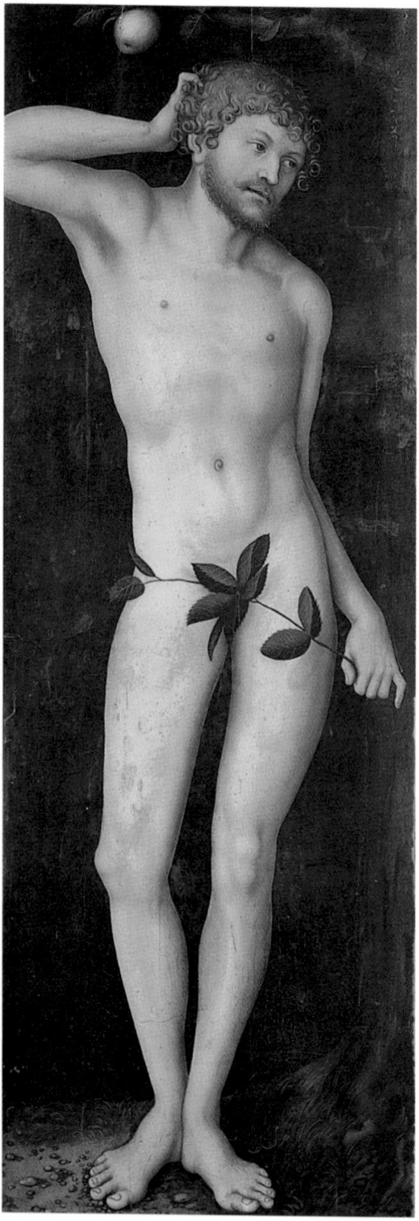

Lukas Cranach the Elder
Adam and Eve

Signed and dated 1528
Oil on wood
172×63; 167×61
Inv. nos. 1459, 1458
In the Uffizi before 1794
Restored: 1999

This representation of Adam and Eve before their sin dates back to a famous etching made by Dürer in 1504. Three years later, this same German master repeated the subject on two panel paintings now in Prado (209×81), two contemporary copies of which (212×85, inv. nos. 8432-8433) attributed to Baldung Grien, a pupil of Dürer's in Nurenberg, are on show in this room of the Uffizi. In these two paintings, Adam and Eve have not yet bitten the apple and appear as nude and beautiful as classical divinities. More than twenty years later, Lukas Cranach, who had worked with this theme since at least 1510 (*Adam and Eve* now in the Warsaw Museum, 59×44), painted the parents of humankind on the two panels shown here, which were part of the grandducal Florentine collections in 1688. Here also the couple are portrayed before their sin, their nudity scantly covered by small branches from the apple tree. Cranach, however influenced by Dürer's art, developed an original style following his Protestant ideas which ignored the classical influences of his master. A friend of Luther, whom he portrayed on various occasions, including with his wife (two small panel paintings from his workshop dated 1529 are in this room, nos. 1160 and 1139), Cranach was also a painter at the Court of Saxony and today is considered the 'official' artist of the Reformation. Also from his workshop come the *Portraits of Martin Luther* and *Philip Melanchton* (1543, inv. nos. 512 and 472) and the *Portraits of the Electors of Saxon* (1533, inv. nos. 1149 and 1150), also in this room.

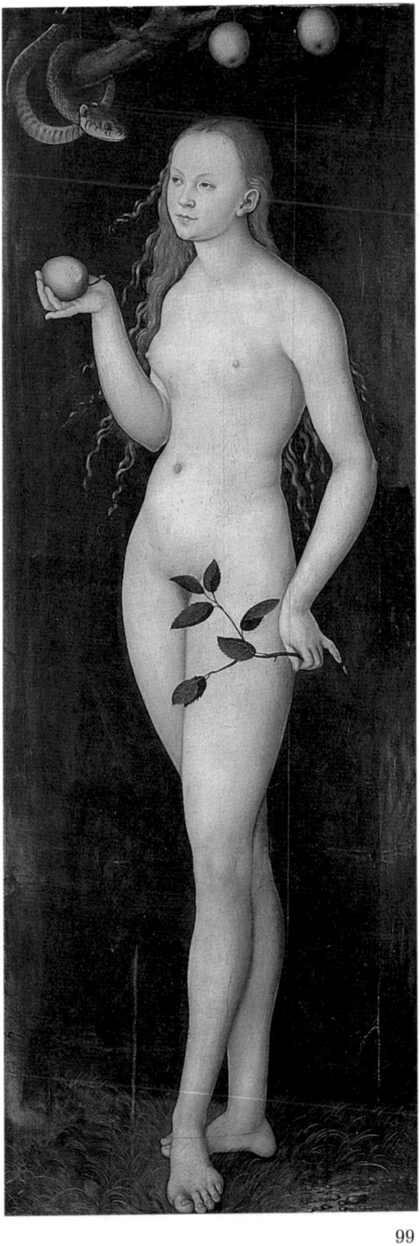

Room 21 ◆ Giambellino and Giorgione

As in the previous two rooms adjoining the Tribune and the two to follow, this room was part of the space that Ferdinand I dedicated to his collection of armoury in 1588. Ferdinand, who succeeded his brother Francesco as Grand Duke, took great interest in the Gallery and in increasing his collections, amongst which that of weapons and armour is particularly valuable. The frescoes on the ceiling, for Ludovico Buti is principally responsible, represent battles and grotesque *motifs showing Indians and tropical fauna and flora, displaying the expansionist tendencies of the Medici towards the New World, and particularly Mexico, from whence many pieces in their collection came, formerly kept in what is now Room 24. Today, Room 21 contains various masterpieces by artists active in the second half of the 15th century and the early 16th century: Venetians such as Giovanni Bellini and Giorgione, and artists from Ferrara such as Cosmè Tura.*

Ludovico Buti
Grotesque-style Ceiling with Battles and "Mexican" Subjects

1588

Fresco with retouches in tempera

Giovanni Bellini known as Giambellino
Allegory

Variously dated between 1487 and 1501
Oil on wood
73×119
Inv. no. 903
In the Uffizi since 1795

Giovanni Bellini, one of the most important Venetian masters of the late 15th century, produced in this work one of the most fascinating enigmas in all of western painting. Many possible theories have been advanced concerning the symbolic meaning of this unusual *Allegory*. The painting is full of saints and animals including a centaur, set in a peaceful, acquatic landscape, rich in interesting detail to be noted and explored.

Defined as "unique and disturbingly inexplicable", it is difficult to date precisely over the long development of Bellini's career. On the terrace is a kind of *hortus conclusus*, or sacred enclosure, where the Virgin is flanked by two women. She is the only one seated with the exception of the Infant Jesus to whom a child (perhaps the infant St John) offers a fallen apple from a small tree (perhaps the Tree of Life) being shaken by another child in the centre of the composition, which is dominated by a chequered pavement in a design which may allude to the Cross. To the right are two saints, Jerome (or Job) and Sebastian.

At the balustrade is St Paul driving away an Asian man (a heretic?) with his sword, and St Peter (or St Joseph). On the opposite side of the bank, to the right, is St Anthony's hermitage marked with a cross.

The most likely interpretations are that it was either an allegory of Redemption or the life of man, which may identify the painting as one requested by Isabella d'Este for her studiolo in Mantua.

Giorgione and Assistance
Moses Undergoing Trial by Fire

c. 1502-1505
Oil on wood
89×72
Inv. no. 945
In the Uffizi since 1795

Like its companion painting beside it, this small panel painting, was listed in 1692 as part of the patrimony of the Grand Duchess of Tuscany at Poggio Imperiale. Moses is represented here as a newborn baby, whom Pharaoh, sitting on his throne, is subjecting to trial by burning coals in order to verify why the baby had taken the crown from his head. This rare episode is narrated in Jewish medieval texts such as the *Shemot Rabbà* which recount legends and moral teachings on biblical figures and events.

Giorgione and Assistance
The Judgement of Solomon

c. 1502-1508
Oil on wood
89×72
Inv. no. 947
In the Uffizi since 1795

This scene comes from the Bible (III, 3, *Kings*): in the place of the Pharaoh from the other painting, here Solomon sits on the throne; various characters are awaiting his sentence, including a warrior holding a still-living child by the arm, contested by the two women who disown the other newborn child, already dead and lying on the ground. Here, as in the panel next to it, the general layout and landscape are certainly by Giorgione, while certain weaker figures can probably be attributed to his helpers.

HANS MEMLING
Portrait of an Unknown Man

c. 1470
Oil on wood
37×26
Inv. no. 1102
In the Uffizi since 1836

Memling, one of the most celebrated portraitists of his time, influenced many Italian artists, among them Perugino.
They may have seen his works in Florence, sent by the Portinari to the church of Santa Maria Nuova, along with the large triptych by Van der Goes (exhibited in Room 10-14).

HANS MEMLING
Portrait of an Unknown Man

c. 1490
Oil on wood
35×25
Inv. no. 1101
In the Uffizi since 1863

The work is one of a series by the Flemish painter Hans Memling, who also carried out portraits of various members of the Portinari family in Bruges, as demonstrated in this room by *The Man Praying* which has been identified as Benedetto Portinari. This was part of a triptych with *Saint Benedict* (also exhibited here).

ALBRECHT ALTDORFER
Martyrdom of Saint Florian

c. 1516-1525

Oil on wood
76.4×67.2
Inv. Dep. no. 4
In the Uffizi since 1914
Restored: 1980

Painted by one of the most important representatives of the 16th century Danube school, this panel painting is part of an altarpiece portraying episodes from the life of the saint. Probably from the church of St Florian near Linz (Austria), it is now divided amongst various museums (one panel painting, the *Leave-taking of St Florian*, is exhibited in this room). Under a cloudy sky, this fragment showing a landscape is particularly effective, with its foreshortening from beneath a wooden bridge upon which the crowded scene of the martyrdom is taking place.

Hans Holbein the Younger
Portrait of Sir Richard Southwell

Dated 1536
Oil on wood
47.5×38
Inv. no. 1087
In the Uffizi before 1638

Requested as a gift in 1620 by Cosimo de' Medici II from Thomas Howard, Duke of Arundel, this work dates back to the mature phase of the great portraitist from Augsburg, who was active for a long time at the English court. Holbein investigates the man's face with scrupulous accuracy, and pauses over every fold of his clothing. The original ebony frame of this painting is lost; beneath the painting four silver medallions remain displaying the coats of arms of the Medici, of the Arundels, of Southwell, and the name of the painter.

This is the end of the series of rooms parallel to the First Corridor and, like the previous two, formed part of the original armoury decorated with frescoes by Ludovico Buti (1588). On the ceiling are illustrations showing the manufacture of arms, of particular interest for the portrayal of the workshops of the period, with swords, lances and breastplates being forged. Other sections show cannons, the making of gunpowder, and the building of a fort. Today the room contains works by the Emilian painter Correggio and the Paduan Andrea Mantegna; by the latter we find the so-called Triptych *illustrated in these pages, and a tiny panel painting of the* Madonna of the Rocks *(c.1489), which may have belonged to Francesco de' Medici.*

Andrea Mantegna
Adoration of the Magi

c. 1462

Tempera on wood
77×75
Inv. no. 910
In the Uffizi since 1632

This panel showing the *Adoration of the Magi*, painted separately on a slightly concave surface, was inserted in 1827 into a non-original frame to form an arbitrary triptych together with two other panels; these are illustrated and described on the following pages.

Andrea Mantegna
The Ascension (left) and *The Circumcision* (right)

c. 1462-1470
Tempera on wood
86×42.5 (each panel)
Inv. no. 910
In the Uffizi since 1632

The panels with *The Ascension* and *The Circumcision* illustrated here have been joined arbitrarily in a triptych to an *Adoration* (previous page), in a rich 19th century frame. Owned by the Medici from at least 1587, the three paintings had first been the property of the Gonzaga family. They are generally believed to be identified with the "small but very beautiful scenes with figures", mentioned by Vasari in 1568 as decorations for the chapel of the Castle of San Giorgio in Mantua. There are in fact letters going back to the year 1459 from Ludovico Gonzaga to Mantegna inviting him to his court. This period is getting close to the likely commencement of at least one of the three panels. The paintings are diverse both in style and size, and are very probably from different periods. This may have been the painter's first commission from the Mantuan court, where he was later to paint a fresco in

the famous *Room of the Bride and Groom*.
By the middle of the 15th century, the Mantuan artistic scene was already adopting a taste for the classical, owing to the presence of sculptors like Pisanello, Donatello, and architects such as Leon Battista Alberti and Luca Fancelli from Fiesole. It is no coincidence that Mantegna was invited to take part, as amongst northern Italian painters he was one of the most receptive to the classical revival. This is especially evident in the right-hand panel, whose scene is set in a sumptuous polychrome marble interior with classical-style reliefs, so different from the *Ascension* painting, which is dominated by a rugged and rocky landscape. In the *Adoration of the Magi*, the range of brilliant colours, typical of the Lombard-Venetian culture, is combined with a powerfully scenic composition. The concave form of the panel's wooden support suggests that the painting was perhaps destined for the rear wall of the chapel of the Castle of San Giorgio, creating a niche over the altar. The vertical panels may instead have been inserted into gold frames on the other walls of the room.

Correggio
The Virgin Adoring the Christ Child

c. 1524-1526
Oil on canvas
82×68.3
Inv. no. 1453
In the Uffizi since 1617
Restored: 2007

A gift in 1617 from the Duke of Mantua to Cosimo de' Medici II, this work was immediately placed in the Tribune, where it remained until the end of the 19th century.
With poetic foreshortening, lit perhaps by the light of a sunset, the young Madonna kneels and gazes adoringly at her Child, in a scene of tranquil and effective balance. The work dates to the middle phase of the Emilian artist's activity, shortly preceding the "greatly foreshortened" fresco decoration of the cupola in Parma Cathedral.

Room 24 ◆ Cabinet of Miniatures

This small room contains more than 400 miniatures from the rich grand-ducal collections. Originally named "The Chamber of Idols" with antique bronzes, Mexican objects, and works in gold, the room was then given the name, "Madam's Chamber", and from 1589 contained the jewels of Christine of Lorraine, wife of Ferdinand I. It then housed the Medicean collection of classical gems and cameos which remained there until 1928 (now at the Museo degli Argenti). Today the room has an oval form as desired by the Grand Duke Pietro Leopoldo (1781). Zanobi del Rosso was the architect responsible and Filippo Lucci painted the fresco, Allegory of Fame, *on the vault. The miniatures on display are small portraits from various eras and schools, subsequently mounted into small composits. They come from a great number of collections constituted between 1664 and 1675 by Cardinal Leopoldo de' Medici. The Cardinal was at the same time increasing his collections of self-portraits and drawings. The miniatures were in part purchased by Paolo del Sera, his agent in Venice, and by other intermediaries all over Italy. Some of the pieces are heirlooms while others Leopoldo had done by artists active in Florence. Hung above the pictures are six noteworthy parchments, including reproductions of famous paintings by Raphael and Titian which were once in the Medicean collection.*

Second and Third corridors

The rearrangement of the Second and Third Corridors was carried out at the same time as the restoration of the First Corridor in 1996. With its large glass windows facing the Uffizi Square and the Arno River, the South Corridor (illustrated, right) is famous for its views. Among the sculptures exhibited are the head of the so-called Dying Alexander *from the Hellenistic period and the Roman copy of* Cupid and Psyche. *At the intersection with the East Corridor, the ceilings are painted with frescoes in the* grotesque *style, dating back to Francesco I (1581). Those facing west show the glorification of the Medici family (Nasini and Tonelli) and date back to Cosimo III (1670-1723). Above the windows facing the river are the later portraits of the Giovio Series, which continue into the Third Corridor together with canvas paintings from the 17th to the beginning of the 19th century, spaced alternately with the larger paintings from the Aulic Series, many of which have been restored. On the side of the doors of the Third Corridor hang 50 portraits of the Lorraine dynasty. Following the evidence of an 18th century drawing in the Album of De Greyss, the famous Roman* Wild Boar *has been reinstalled at the end of the corridor towards the Loggia dei Lanzi. This, along with the small replica of a* Farnese Hercules, *is placed beside the* Laocoon *by Baccio Bandinelli (1523), the first copy from the original of the Hellenistic group found in Rome in 1506. All three sculptures were restored in 1994.*

On the left:
FLORENTINE SCHOOL
Grotesque Decoration
(Second Corridor)
c. 1581
Fresco
with tempera
retouches
c. 616×616

The *trompe l'œil* pergolas are bordered with coats of arms of the Medici family, the House of Austria (the first wife of Francesco I was Jean of Austria), and Bianca Cappello, lover and then second wife of the Grand Duke. The emblem of Cappello, who was disliked by the Medicis, was previously covered but later found during restoration.

Wild Boar
(Third Corridor)
First century A.D.
Roman copy from Greek bronze original
Marble, ht. 85, lgth. 151, wth. 129
Inv. 1914 no. 63
In the Uffizi since 1591
Restored: 1994

The *Wild Boar* comes from the house of Paolo Ponti in Rome, where it was documented in 1556. Highly esteemed for its naturalism, the sculpture was damaged by a fire in 1762 and restored immediately afterwards. In 1634, Pietro Tacca made a copy of it for his bronze known as the *Porcellino* (Little Pig), which stands in the Mercato Nuovo.

Room 25, dominated by a masterpiece by Michelangelo, is the first of eleven rooms now dedicated to 16th century painting. In what are now Rooms 25-33, the Grand Duke Ferdinand I in 1588 established workshops for the Minor Guilds and a Foundry for the distillation of perfumes, poisons and antidotes. In the mid-18th century, Rooms 25-26 exhibited medals and gems, and at the end of the century, Venetian paintings of the 15th and the 16th century. Dedicated to 16th century works after the Second World War, this series of rooms has recently acquired a new, rigorously geographical layout which has been helped by the restoration following the 1993 bombing.

MICHELANGELO
Holy Family with the Infant St John the Baptist (*Doni Tondo*)

c. 1506-1508
Contemporaneous frame, carved and gilded, attributed to Marco and Francesco del Tasso
Tempera on wood
diam. 120
170 including the frame
Inv. no. 1456
In the Uffizi (in the Tribune) since 1635
Painting and frame restored in 1985

Rightly considered to be the most important and enigmatic painting of the 16th century, the *Doni Tondo* is the only example of Michelangelo's painting preserved in Florence. It may also be the only painting on a movable support which can definitely be attributed to him. Executed for the Flo-

rentine merchant Agnolo Doni and his wife Maddalena Strozzi, possibly on the occasion of the birth of their daughter Maria (September 8, 1507), it was certainly painted after January 1506 when the *Laocoon* was found in Rome, a sculpture from which Michelangelo took the pose of the nude sitting behind St Joseph.
It is no coincidence that the postures of the nudes are derived from many other classical sculptures known at the time. Michelangelo was in fact strongly influenced by classical statuary, which he studied with great care. This unusual *Holy Family* in striking tones, a prelude to Mannerist art, shows three almost sculptural figures in the foreground in a strange and serpentine composition. The figure of the Virgin is taking Jesus from (or offering him to) St Joseph. She is counterbalanced by five young nudes behind a small wall, who lean or sit on a balustrade, beyond which a simple landscape fades into the horizon. The meaning of this work is still uncertain; it may be inspired by the Biblical passages which refer to the birth and baptism of Christ, hinted at by the bust of the infant St John to the right, and the five round lunettes on the frame showing Christ, angels and prophets.

MARIOTTO ALBERTINELLI
Visitation

Dated on the pillars 1503
Oil on wood
232.5×146.5; 23×149.5 (predella with *Annunciation, Adoration of the Child, Circumcision*, not shown)
Inv. nos. 1587, 1586

Panel in the Uffizi since 1786, predella since 1794
Restored: 1995

The masterpiece of this painter, famous for the combination of strength and softness in his style, was formerly in the church of San Michele in Palchetto. Whilst the painting has classical elements, shown by the architectural composition and the harmonious balance created in the meeting between Mary and Elizabeth, it also anticipates the *Doni Tondo* in its almost metallic colours newly evident after restoration.

Ridolfo del Ghirlandaio (attr.)
Cover of a Portrait

c. 1510
Oil on wood
73×50.3
Inv. no. 6042
In the Uffizi since 1867
Restored: 2008

In the beginning of the 19th century, this *tirella*, then attributed to Leonardo, covered the portrait of the *Veiled Woman*, exhibited here under attribution to Ridolfo del Ghirlandaio. This small panel, very probably painted by the Florentine master famous for his grotesque decorations, did perhaps from the outset cover the portrait of a woman carried out by Ghirlandaio. The classical inscription with the motto SUA CUIQUE PERSONA (To each his own mask) comes from Seneca and Quintilian.

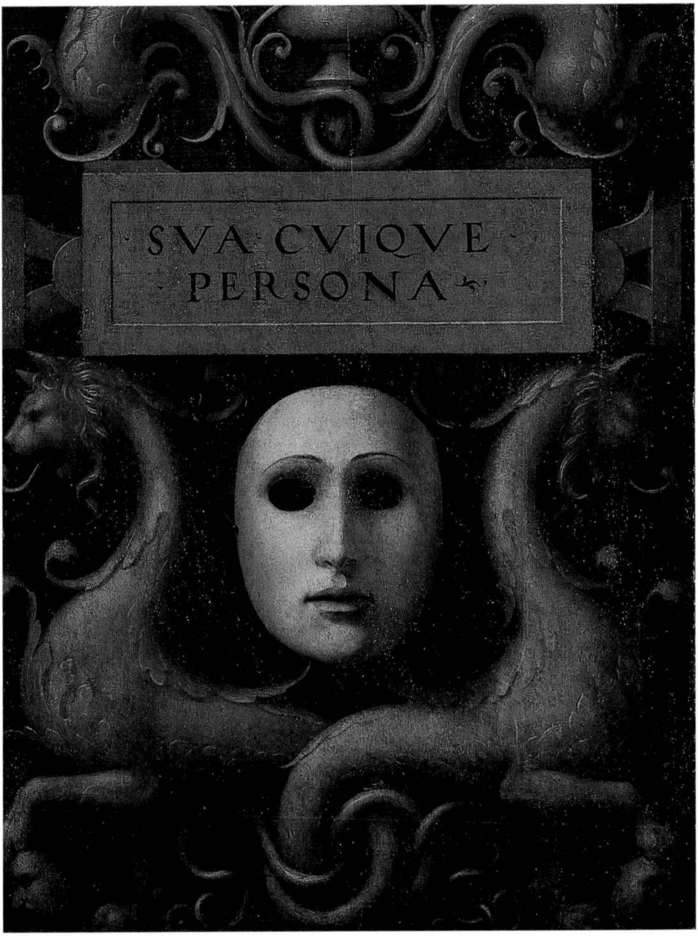

Fra Bartolomeo
Annunciation
(recto)
Presentation at the Temple and Nativity
(verso)

c. 1497

Oil on wood, 19.5×9; 18×9
Inv. no. 1477
In the Tribune since 1589, from the collection of Cosimo de' Medici I (1568)

These panels were painted, almost in miniature, for Piero del Pugliese (1430-1498), an important figure in Florentine history. They were to serve as shutters enclosing a bas-relief of the Madonna and Child by Donatello (London, Victoria & Albert Museum, c. 1440). The unusual tabernacle, with its sculpture which is much older than the paintings themselves (which were later reduced in size to readapt the piece subsequently deprived of its relief), confirms the refined taste of the owner, who was also a patron of Botticelli, Filippino Lippi, Piero di Cosimo, and perhaps Pollaiolo.

RAFFAELLO SANZIO
Madonna of the Goldfinch

c. 1505-1506
Tempera on wood
107×77.2
Inv. no. 1447
In the Uffizi since 1666
Restored: 2008

Painted for the merchant Lorenzo Nasi at the time of his marriage to Sandra Canigiani (1505), the panel was damaged in 1547 when the house on Via de' Bardi collapsed. The young Raphael, in Florence from the year 1504 (he also worked later for Nasi's brother-in-law), here experimented for the first time with a group of figures centred in the foreground, against a backdrop of a Leonardesque landscape. The Virgin is seated with a book in one hand and her Son between her knees. He caresses the goldfinch offered to him by the infant St John.

Raffaello Sanzio
Pope Leo X with Cardinals Giulio de' Medici and Luigi de' Rossi

1518

Oil on wood
155.5×119.5
Inv. 1912 no. 40
In the Tribune in 1589
Restored: 1996

The portrait of Leo X (Giovanni de' Medici, 1475-1521, elected Pope in 1513) arrived in Florence from Rome in 1518. It was later praised by Vasari for its figures which are "not fake, but painted in full relief", for the "rustling and shining" damask robe, for the "soft and realistic" fur linings, for the golden knob on the chair which reflects "the light from the windows, the Pope's shoulders, and the surrounding room". The recent restoration has given rise to the theory that the two cardinals may be an addition by another hand.

ANDREA DEL SARTO
The Madonna of the Harpies

Signed and dated 1517

Tempera on wood
207×178
Inv. no. 1577
In the Tribune since 1785
Restored: 1984

Begun in 1515 for the Sisters of San Francesco de' Macci, the painting was not completed within the time and manner required. Together with the St John the Evangelist, requested in the contract, a St Francis was added beside the Virgin and Child instead of St Bonaventure.

The work takes its name, following a mistake of Vasari's, from the monsters ("Harpies") in bas-relief on the base. It now appears that they are locusts, according to the complex theological significance of the painting, alluding to the ninth chapter of St John's Apocalypse.

ROSSO FIORENTINO (e RIDOLFO DEL GHIRLANDAIO?)
Madonna with Child and Saints (Madonna dello Spedalingo)

1518

Tempera on wood; 172×141
Inv. no. 3190
In the Uffizi since 1900
Restored: 1995

In 1518 Leonardo Buonafé, rector of the Santa Maria Nuova hospital (the 'Spedalingo'), commissioned an altarpiece for the church of Ognissanti. According to Vasari, the sketch of the painting was refused by Buonafé, because the saints looked like "devils", customary for Rosso, who, in the end, "sweetened" the "bitter and desperate expressions" painted in the oil sketches. The altarpiece with its very unusual figures did not reach Ognissanti, and the initial painting of Buonafé's namesake St Leonard was then substituted by a St Stephen.

PONTORMO
The Supper at Emmaus

Dated on the scroll below on the right 1525
Oil on canvas
230×173
Inv. no. 8740
In the Uffizi since 1948
Restored: 1994

This panel was painted for the guest-room of the Charterhouse in Galluzzo south of Florence, where Pontormo had spent a peaceful period of time in 1523. The Apparition of Christ to the Apostles is portrayed with intense spirituality. Inspired by a Dürer etching, an artist whose work Pontormo often studied at this time, the painting nevertheless reveals an independent style, theatrical in its surprising touches of light and detailed observation of everyday life (the friar to the left is the elder Leonardo Buonafé, then prior of the Charterhouse).

Bronzino
Holy Family with the Infant St John (The Panciatichi Holy Family)

c. 1538-1540

Tempera on wood
116.9×93.5
Inv. no. 8377
In the Uffizi since 1919

Painted for the Panciatichi family, as shown by their emblem on the flag flying on the tower to the top left of the painting, this is one of the most interesting compositions of Bronzino, a man of culture, an author of superb verses and a close friend of Pontormo. His style is very original, whilst still remaining in line with his role as portrait painter to the court and the cream of Florentine society. The patron of this work is probably Bartolomeo Panciatichi whose portrait, alongside that of his wife, hangs in the Tribune.

Titian
Flora

c. 1515-1517
Oil on canvas
79.7×63.5
Inv. no. 1462
In the Uffizi since 1793
Restored: 1993

This much-admired, sensual painting was in Alfonso Lopez's collection in Amsterdam; it arrived at the Uffizi in 1641 in an exchange with the Imperial Gallery of Vienna.

This is almost certainly a portrait of a young bride, who rather timidly reveals her breast with one hand, whilst with the other, on which she wears a barely visible wedding band, she holds a bouquet of flowers.

This beauty with her long, loosened hair and intense expression represents Flora, Goddess of Fertility.

TITIAN
The Venus of Urbino

1538

Oil on canvas
119×165
Inv. no. 1437
In Florence since 1631, from the inheritance of Victoria della Rovere, wife of Ferdinand de' Medici II
In the Uffizi since 1736
Restored: 1996

Commissioned in 1538 from the Venetian master by Guidubaldo della Rovere, the Duke of Urbino, this is one of the most famous erotic images of all time, a cultural icon. A young girl with blond hair flowing loosely over her shoulders, looks knowingly but allusively at the spectator. She is completely naked, lying on a luxurious bed with rumpled sheets; her left hand resting over the pubic area as if to hide it is in fact ambiguously inviting. In her right hand she holds a small posy of roses, a symbol of love reiterated by the myrtle plant

on the window-sill. The little dog sleeping on the bed, symbolises fidelity, a tender and reassuring note in the scene; this carries on in the background, where two maid-servants are looking for clothes in a rich bridal chest, in a fading sunset. The recent restoration has recovered Titian's typical colour scheme, highlighting the detail of fabric, of flesh tones, and even the small pearl shining on the ear of the young bride. Awaited impatiently by Duke Guidubaldo, who more than once asked the Ambassador of Urbino in Venice for news about it, the painting was to serve as an instructive "model" for Giulia Varano, the Duke's extremely young bride.

SEBASTIANO DEL PIOMBO
The death of Adonis
(whole and detail)

c. 1512
Oil on canvas, 189×285
Inv. no. 916
In the Uffizi since 1798
Restored: 1994
(restored in 1987 prior to the 1993 bombing)

Painted in Rome for the patron Agostino Chigi, who since 1511 had been asking the Venetian artist to fresco his villa, the Farnesina, this canvas was in the Pitti Palace in 1587, and in 1675 in the collection of Cardinal Leopoldo. Ripped in 1993 and restored immediately, it is a symbol of the Uffizi's renewal after the bomb.
Possibly identifiable as the painting with "mostly nude and beautiful figures" in a 1520 inventory of the Villa Farnesina, it is filled with cultural allusions and references. The subject is inspired by the desperation of Venus at the death of Adonis (left). Venus sits naked in the foreground in a posture presumably taken from the classical *Boy Removing a Thorn from his Foot* (see Archaeological Collections). The painting hides a moralistic meaning around the lament of *Venice-Venusia* (Venus = Venusia), the city which appears in the background with its famous monuments: the Ducal Palace, the domes of the Palatine Basilica, the Clock Tower, and the Vecchie Procuratie.
In this mythological evocation, Venice appears to be absorbed by the seductions of sensual beauty and is destined to death and putrefaction (Adonis killed by the boar).

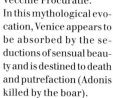

Dosso Dossi
Witchcraft
or *Allegory of Hercules*

c. 1535-1538
Oil on canvas
143×144
Inv. Palatina no. 148
In the Uffizi since 1950

Acquired in Siena in 1665 for Cardinal Leopoldo, this is the masterpiece of the late period of Dossi's career, which began in 1514 at the Ferrara court and later moved to other cities. The meaning of the unusual subject matter is still doubtful. It is described in Cardinal Leopoldo's inventory as "the painting with portraits of the clowns of the Dukes of Ferrara".
Rich in allusions and marked by a satirical note in the twisted faces, almost caricatures, it was perhaps dedicated to Ercole d'Este, the Duke of Ferrara.

Parmigianino
Madonna with Child and Saints (The St Zacchariah Madonna)

c. 1530
Oil on wood
75.5×60
Inv. no. 1328
In the Tribune since 1605
Restored: 1994

Painted in Bologna, possibly for Bonifacio Gozzadini, the panel shows the half-length figure of St Zacchariah in the foreground, in a three-quarter pose, carrying a large open book.
In front of him the Madonna sits and smiles, with the Child being embraced by a semi-nude infant St John who is portrayed as a cupid.
Behind this group is a fine and sensual Mary Magdalen holding her vase of ointment, her breast partially covered by her hair. A livid sky in the background hangs over the mountains; distant cities reminiscent of Roman times can also be made out, reinforced in the middle ground by ancient ruins and a classical building with a Greek inscription.
The painting is dated to the period of the artist's stay in Bologna, who had left Rome in 1527 after a period of three years

PARMIGIANINO
The Madonna of the Long Neck

c. 1534-1539

Oil on wood
219×135
Inv. Palatina no. 230
In the Uffizi since 1948

Painted for the Servi church in Parma. The inscription on the step beneath the column shows that this work remained unfinished, and in fact the painting was found in the artist's studio at his death at the age of thirty-seven in 1540. On the right side of the painting, famous for the refined, exaggerated length of its figures, is the foot of a saint who was supposed to be alongside Jerome who holds a scroll.

LUDOVICO MAZZOLINO
Slaughter of the Innocents

c. 1525
Oil on wood
49×59
Inv. no. 1350
In the Uffizi since 1704

This crowded and lively composition is a replica by the artist of the small panel now in the Galleria Doria Pamphilj in Rome (c. 1521); it dates to Mazzolino's mature period. The rather mannered scene takes place against the background of a loggia which opens to the right onto a nordic-style landscape. Mazzolino was active in Ferrara from the year 1504, when he was commissioned by Ercole d'Este for a series of fresco decorations in the church of Santa Maria degli Angeli. These frescoes were lost in a fire in 1604.
The artist is open to the new Venetian "colourism" and particularly to Giorgione. His work is also influenced by northern painting, mainly that of Dürer, a painter studied by many Italian artists thanks to the wide circulation of his etchings. Mazzolino's style is however marked by a "capricious" and bizarre imagination that fitted in well with the eclectic culture of a city like Ferrara.
In this small room, dedicated to Emilian 16th century painters, are other paintings by the same master, all in the small dimensions through which Ludovico Mazzolino best expressed his talent.

PAOLO VERONESE
The Martyrdom of Saint Justine

c. 1570-1575
Oil on canvas
103×113
Inv. no. 946
In the Tribune in 1704
Restored: 1988

This canvas by Veronese was formerly part of the Canonici di Ferrara Collection (1632), and later belonged to Paolo Del Sera, an intermediary in Venice for Cardinal Leopoldo de' Medici who then bought it from him around 1654.
The subject of the painting is the same as that of a great and more animated altarpiece possibly executed by Paolo Veronese together with his brother for the Basilica of Santa Giustina in Padua (c. 1574), for which a preparatory drawing exists (Chatsworth, Collection of the Duke of Devonshire). Veronese, who in 1573 underwent a trial for taking too much liberty with his depiction of holy themes, was a master at creating spectacular scenes filled with light.
Further canvases of his displayed in this room come from Cardinal Leopoldo's collections: an airy, monumental *Annunciation* (1556, inv. no. 899) and the *Holy Family* from Widman House (c. 1561, inv. no. 1433), a painting dominated by the imposing blonde figure of St Catherine.

JACOPO TINTORETTO
Leda and the Swan
(whole and detail)
c. 1550-1560
Oil on canvas, 167×221
Inv. no. 3084
In the Uffizi since 1893
Restored: 1994

Having passed through various collections, this canvas is a donation from Arturo De Noè Walker. In an interior embellished with pets (a parrot in an aviary, a cat staring threateningly at a caged duck, and a little dog who is perhaps jealous of a swan), the painting shows the mythical, sensual Leda, dressed only in pearls, caressing Jove, who has transformed himself into a swan to seduce her. The restorations have clarified that the presence of the maidservant is not arbitrary as far as its prototype (in the Uffizi since 1989, inv. no. 9946) is concerned. This, now also restored, is missing the figure because of a cut in the canvas.

GIORGIO VASARI
Vulcan's Forge

c. 1564
Oil on copper
38×28
Inv. no. 1558
In the Uffizi since 1589

Perhaps originally in the Tribune, this small copperplate, along with other works in the enlarged and modernised corridor, exemplifies Mannerist painting of the European Court in the second half of the 16th century. In the forge, Vulcan, god of subterranean fires, is in the foreground. Symbol of genius, he is chiselling a shield showing Capricorn, the astrological sign of Francesco I, and Aries, the ascendant of his father, Cosimo, holding up the world. Above are the Three Graces, emblems of the Art of Drawing, modelling for four nude artists.

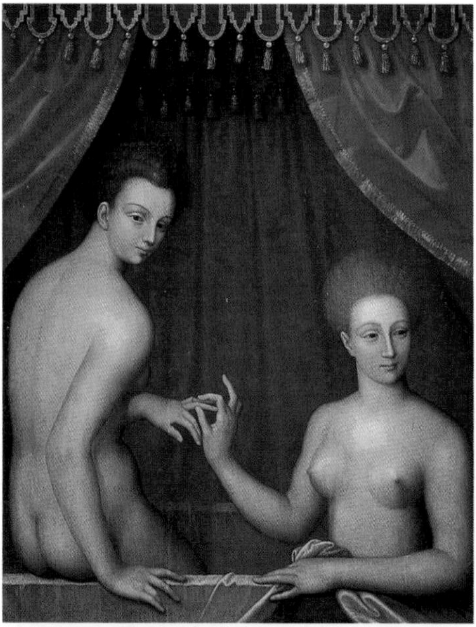

SCHOOL OF FONTAINEBLEAU
Two Women Bathing

Last quarter
of the 16th century
Oil on wood; 129×97
Inv. no. 9958
In the Uffizi since 1989

It is not known who the two women in this painting are. Portrayed in different versions, they are generally identified as Gabrielle d'Estrées (1571-1599), lover of Henri IV, and her sister, the Duchess of Villars.
They nonetheless coincide with the standards of ideal beauty held by the lyrical 16th century, with white, yellow, and red as the dominant colours.

FRANÇOIS CLOUET
François I of France on Horseback

c. 1540
Tempera on wood
27.5×22.5
Inv. no. 987
In the Uffizi since 1796

This small court portrait arrived in Florence in 1589 when Christine of Lorraine, wife of Ferdinand I, inherited it from her grandmother Caterina de' Medici, Queen of France, together with miniatures executed in Clouet's workshop, portraying Henri II and relatives (they are illustrated on page 12 in a 19th century arrangement).

Room 34 ◆ Lombard Painting of the 16th century

Lorenzo Lotto
The Chastity of Susannah

Signed and dated 1517
Oil on wood
66×50
Inv. no. 9491
In the Uffizi since 1975

A man of culture, a wanderer and a loner, Lotto painted the biblical episode of Susannah being harassed while bathing by two old men whom she drives away. The scene, shown from above to reveal an apparently traditional backdrop beyond the wall, instead shows two old men hidden in the branches of a tree spying on Susannah as she walks to the bath. On didactic scrolls, as if in anticipation of our modern comic strips, Susannah declares that she does not want to sin, while the old men take their revenge by accusing her of adultery with a young man.

GIOVAN BATTISTA MORONI
Portrait of Pietro Secco Suardo
Signed "Io Bap. Moronus p." and dated 1563, under the writing:
ET QUID VOLO NISI UT ARDEAT
Oil on canvas
183×104
Inv. no. 906
In the Uffizi since 1797

Known for the psychological realism of his portraits, Moroni, a painter from Bergamo, here portrays his countryman Suardo, Ambassador of Venice from 1545. A few precise brush strokes render the essential elements of this interior: the deformed shadow on the square pavement and the window view. On a base stands the burning brazier, alluding to the family motto written below, taken from St Luke's Gospel (12:49): "How I wish it [the fire] were blazing already". The Latin words [NI]S[I] U[T] ARDE[AT] conceal in acrostic the horseman's surname.

FEDERICO BAROCCI
The Madonna of the People

Signed and dated 1579
Oil on wood
359×272
Inv. no. 751
In the Uffizi since 1787
Restored: 1995

Barocci did many preparatory drawings for this large altarpiece painted for a church in Arezzo. Christ, through the intercession of the Virgin, is blessing the some of the populace, who are portrayed with lively detail as they bustle around with their daily lives.

The work, created in an environment of renewed spirituality, immediately drew many admired Tuscan artists to the church; several of their paintings are in the new display in this room (among them Cigoli, Empoli, Santi di Tito, Alessandro Allori).

PIETER PAUL RUBENS
Isabella Brandt

c. 1625
Oil on wood
86×62
Inv. no. 779
In the Uffizi since 1773

"A very good companion [...] completely good, completely honest and beloved for her virtues": Rubens remembers his first wife, immediately after her death in 1626. Often portrayed by him, Isabella is shown here half-length, shortly before her death, against a shady background of a curtain and a column.
The portrait was given as a gift in 1705 by the Palatine Elector of the Rhine Johann Wilhelm to his brother-in-law Ferdinando de' Medici, who called it a "work of genius" from the "famous brush" of Rubens.

DIEGO VELÁZQUEZ AND WORKSHOP
Philip IV of Spain on Horseback

c. 1645
Oil on canvas
338×267
Inv. no. 792
In the Uffizi since 1753
Restored: 1995

This portrait, typical of the Spanish court, was in Madrid in 1651, under the care of the Marquis Eliche (he died in Naples in 1687). It is partly taken from a Rubens painting (c. 1628), known from a description, which was destroyed in Madrid in 1734. Whilst in the original the king was twenty-two years old, here the face is taken from a portrait by Velázquez (1645, now in the New York Frick Collection). The restored canvas reveals the hand of the Spanish painter in the face of the king, on the head of the horse, and in the masterly brushwork around the figures.

PIETER PAUL RUBENS
Triumph

1627-1630
Oil on canvas
383×696
Inv. no. 729
Restored: 2000

Like the Battle, the enormous canvas of the *Triumph*, now returned to the Uffizi after exemplary restoration, has an intriguing history. Both works, inspired by the life of Henri IV, King of France and Navarre, formed part of a series left unfinished in 1630. At the death of Rubens in 1640 the two paintings were still in his studio at Antwerp.
Maria de' Medici, the King's widow, had commissioned the Flemish artist, who may have been present at the royal wedding, celebrated by proxy in Florence in 1600, to paint a commemorative series of battles, sieges and triumphs. The series

was to accompany the scenes from the life of the Queen, painted by Rubens from 1622 to 1625 for the Luxembourg Palace in Paris.
Diplomatic and political problems (Maria was confined to Compiègne and then exiled) prevented the second project from being carried out.
After the painter's death the canvases now in the Uffizi went to the collection of the Antwerp Canon Fréderic Lancelot, at Cambrai.
Although the painter Charles Le Brun tried to buy them for the King of France, it was Apollonio Bassetti, secretary of Cosimo III de' Medici, who managed to obtain them. In 1687 they arrived in Italy from Antwerp, at the port of Livorno, wound in great rolls to protect them, and from there were transported to Florence.

The Niobe Room, has been restored in 2008 after the severe damage it suffered before the 1993 bombing. This 18th century room was planned by Pietro Leopoldo, who put the architect Gaspare Maria Paoletti in charge of displaying a group of classical sculptures. Found in the 16th century in a vineyard in Rome near the Lateran, they recall the myth of Niobe, destroyed with her sons by Apollo and Diana. This sensational discovery was announced in a letter of 1583 written by the sculptor and restorer Valerio Cioli to the secretary of the Grand Duke Francesco I. After several months the statues were acquired by the Grand Duke's brother, Ferdinand, then Cardinal in Rome, who restored them and took them to the Villa Medici. Five years later he sent casts of the sculptures to Florence, which were displayed in the Gallery until Pietro Leopoldo, as mentioned, brought them to Tuscany in 1770. The restoration of the first group (more pieces arrived later) was entrusted to Innocenzo Spinazzi and completed in 1776; by 1795 the statues were on display in the neoclassical room, a space adorned with stuccoes and decorative reliefs.

Running Niobian

c. 130 BC

Pentelic marble, ht. 181
Inv. sculture 1914 no. 300
In the Uffizi since 1795

CARAVAGGIO
Bacchus

Variously dated c. 1596-1600

Oil on canvas
98×85
Inv. no. 5312
In the Uffizi from uncertain date, brought out of store in 1916

NEW ROOMS (FIRST FLOOR)

The famous *Bacchus* may date from the period when Caravaggio was working for Cardinal del Monte (c.1595-1600), a man of culture, who may have ordered the painting as a gift for Ferdinando de' Medici, as he did with the *Medusa*.
The face of the young god of wine is thought to be a portrait of the Sicilian painter Mario Monnitti, who lived with Caravaggio in Rome for some time.
The Dionysian myth, here loaded with philosophical and religious symbols, is portrayed with sensuality and crude realism: the reddened cheeks, the moist lips, the dirty fingernails and the wormeaten, half-rotten fruit.

CARAVAGGIO
Sacrifice of Isaac

Variously dated from 1592 to 1604
Oil on canvas
104×135
Inv. no. 4659
In the Uffizi since 1917

NEW ROOMS (FIRST FLOOR)

Caravaggio, inspired by Genesis, here shows an angel stopping Abraham who in obedience to God is about to sacrifice his son Isaac. Beside the head of the boy, who is shouting desperately, is the ram sent by God to substitute him in the sacrifice. Whilst in the biblical text the angel speaks to Abraham from the sky, here he comes down to the ground to stay his hand directly. The scene, painted with fine strokes of light against a landscape showing a serene Venetian influence, prefigures the sacrifice of Christ and symbolises obedience and faith in accordance with the climate of renewed spirituality of the time. The chronology of this canvas is still doubtful: it was given as a gift to the Uffizi by John F. Murray, son of the pre-Raphaelite painter. Its provenance is also uncertain, as it does not correspond to the painting of an unknown subject, for which the Roman Maffeo Barberini paid Caravaggio between 1603 and 1604.
The canvas in the Uffizi, however, does coincide with the "sacrifice of Abraham who holds the knife to the throat of his son who shouts and falls down", painted for the Barberini family according to the writer Giuseppe Bellori in 1672.

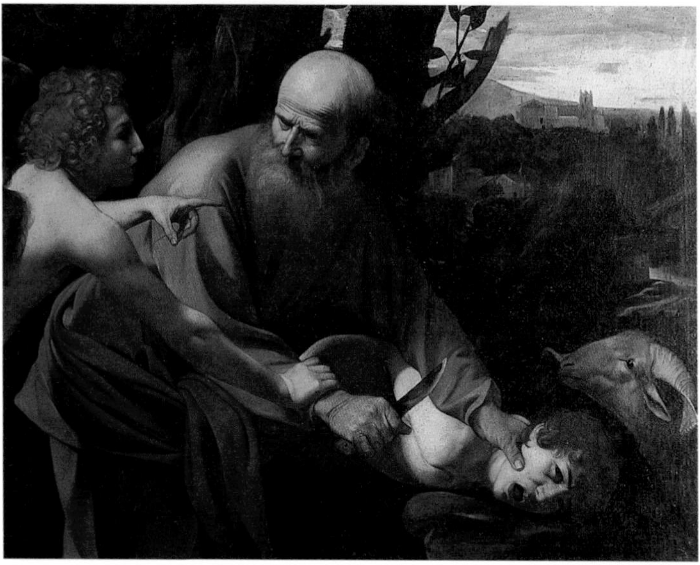

Caravaggio
Medusa

c. 1596-1597
Oil on wood
covered with canvas
diam. 55
Inv. no. 1351
In the Uffizi at least
since 1631
Restored: 2002

New Rooms (First Floor)

Medusa with her head of snakes transformed anyone who looked at her into stone: "Run, for if amazement draws your eyes, /she will turn you into stone". Thus wrote Gaspare Murtola in 1603, admiring the Medusa with her "poisonous hair/armed with a thousand snakes". It was painted in Rome by the "peintre maudit" for the Cardinal Del Monte as a gift to Ferdinando de' Medici. Astonishment is also expressed in the verses of Giovan Battista Marino (1614): "that fierce, harsh Gorgon,/to which they dedicate such horribly/viperish forms/her squalid pomp and frightful locks of hair". In 1631 the convex "rotella" (tournament shield) was on display at the Medicean Armoury, hanging on the arm of an Oriental suit of armour which was a gift from the Shah of Persia to the Grand Duke around the year 1601.

REMBRANDT
Self-Portrait as a Young Man

c. 1634
Oil on wood
62.5×54
Inv. no. 3890
In the Uffizi since 1922
Restored: 2002

ROOM 44 - 17TH CENTURY FLEMISH PAINTERS

Son of a rich miller from Leide, the artist left his native city in 1631 for Amsterdam. There he painted this self-portrait, which already displays confidence and acute psychological investigation. The painting may have been a gift from the Palatine Elector of the Rhine Johann Wilhelm (married to Anna Maria Luisa de' Medici) to the Florentine Gerini family, and was later (1818) acquired by Ferdinand III of Lorraine. The taste for self-portraiture stayed with Rembrandt throughout his career, but especially during his early period.

CANALETTO
View of the Ducal Palace in Venice
(whole and detail)

Before 1755, the year when the Clock Tower underwent modifications absent from this painting

Oil on canvas
51×83
Inv. no. 1334
In the Uffizi since 1798
Restored: 2001

ROOM 45 - THE 18TH CENTURY

One of Canaletto's most often repeated views, the canvas shows the pier and the Riva degli Schiavoni, the Zecca, the Old Library, the Ducal Palace and the Dandolo Palace. The Venetian artist uses a "camera ottica", an optical device he often adopted for his perspective studies.
On the painting at the Uffizi, the foreground is dominated by gondolas and boats with figures busy rowing or throwing ropes. Other versions of the scene instead portray official events such as the celebration of the 'Sensa' at the feast of the Ascension, showing the arrival or departure of the 'Bucintoro', the Doge's galley, festively arrayed.

FRANCISCO GOYA Y LUCIENTES
Portrait of María Teresa, Countess of Chinchón

c. 1798

Oil on canvas; 220×140
Inv. no. 9484
In the Uffizi since 1974

Restored: 2008

ROOM 45 - THE 18TH CENTURY

Goya did portraits of María Teresa, daughter of his patron Luís de Borbón, from the time she was a little girl. In 1783 he also painted his patron's wife riding a horse (Uffizi, inv. no. 9485). In 1797 María married Manuel Godoy, the scheming minister of the King and favourite of the Queen. This was the start of an unhappy life, as can already be guessed from this delicate portrait, in which the young girl's profile is repeated on the medallion bracelet around her wrist. Goya retained close ties of friendship with this woman, and he died like her in exile in France in 1828.

Guido Reni
David with the Head of Goliath

c. 1605
Oil on canvas
222×147
Inv. no. 3830
In the Uffizi since 1913
Restored: 1995

New Rooms (First Floor)

Standing rakishly in a red feathered cap, his figure illuminated by the moonlight and scarcely covered by his rich, fur-trimmed cloak, David leans against a column and surveys the head of the slain giant.
A variation of an earlier painting in the Louvre, there are still echoes of Caravaggio in this work from which the Emilian painter was to detach himself on his return from Rome, in search of an ever more classical style. The painting, damaged during the 1993 bombing, has been restored and returned to the end of the staircase leading down to the Vasari Corridor.

Vasari Corridor

The most spectacular and famous corridor of the world was created in 1565. Giorgio Vasari, the architect of the court, had already been enlarging and restructuring the new Medici residence at Palazzo Vecchio for some time, bringing to an end the great Uffizi project. During the preparations for the magnificent royal wedding of Francesco de' Medici and Jean of Austria, the architect was commissioned by Cosimo I to complete in record time, from March to September 1565, a corridor that was to lead from the Uffizi to Palazzo Pitti, which had been bought in 1549 by Eleonora di Toledo, wife of Cosimo. The Vasari Corridor starts from the west wing of the Uffizi, follows the Arno in an astonishing raised path that passes over the shops of the left parapet of the Ponte Vecchio, overlooks the interior of the church of Santa Felicita, (then the Palatine Chapel), and finally reaches the Boboli Gardens, where works had been going on for some time under the direction of many architects and sculptors. An extraordinary and highly symbolic urban intervention in the ducal city, the Corridor, almost a kilometre long with unique views from its windows and circular apertures, was designed as an exclusive walkway for the Duke, the Princes, and high dignitaries of the court. It was only opened for public use in 1866 when Florence was capital of the Republic. It was then that its real history as a museum began, interrupted for long periods by the damage caused by World War II, the flood (1966), and the bomb (1993). Now restored, the Corridor contains around 800 paintings; on the staircase and in first stretch there are important works from the 17th and 18th century, while on the Ponte Vecchio the most famous collection of self-portraits in the world is displayed, which was begun by Cardinal Leopoldo and is still growing.

Elisabeth Vigée-Le Brun
Self-Portrait

1790
Oil on canvas, 100×81
Inv. no. 1905
In the Uffizi since 1790

In the golden twilight of the Paris *Ancien Régime*, this rich and fashionable artist, the only woman with an academic title, left France at the outbreak of the revolution. Official painter to Marie Antoinette, she portrayed herself painting a portrait of her queen, in this work which had been commissioned by Pietro Leopoldo in Rome: thus creating a self-portrait with a portrait, immediately praised and copied.

Eugène Delacroix
Self-Portrait

c. 1840
Oil on canvas, 66×54
Inv. no. 3914
In the Uffizi since 1912

The artist must build "a mysterious bridge between the soul of the characters and the spectators", wrote Delacroix in his diary. The self-portrait of this artist, a master in his investigation of the human spirit, is stylistically close to another conserved at the Louvre and to the intense *Portrait of Chopin* from 1938 (also at the Louvre).

Contini Bonacossi Collection

The collection, among the most important of the 20th century in Italy, was formed by Alessandro Contini Bonacossi (disappeared 1955), thanks in part to consultation by art critics such as Roberto Longhi and Bernard Berenson. Officially acquired as a donation by the State in 1969, the collection includes dozens of important works by Italian and foreign artists. The dates of the works range from the 13th to the 18th centuries with artists such as Sassetta and Veronese (illustrated here) as well as Andrea del Castagno, Paolo Veneziano, Giovanni Bellini, Savoldo, and El Greco. Until recently, the works were exhibited at the Meridiana pavillon in Palazzo Pitti, but they now find a more appropriate home amongst the Uffizi displays, in specially arranged rooms (temporary entrance from Via Lambertesca).

Sassetta
Madonna of the Snow Altarpiece
(detail of the predella)
c. 1430-1432
Tempera on wood
240×256
Inv. Contini Bonacossi no. 1
In the Uffizi since 1998
Restored: 1998

Painted for the San Bonifacio Chapel in the Siena Cathedral, the title of this altarpiece is inspired by the miraculous snowfall which took place on the Esquiline in Rome on 5th August 358, a day which was then consecrated to St Mary of the Snow. The miracle, pre-announced by the Madonna to the patrician Giovanni, is said to have determined the place where the prestigious basilica of Santa Maria Maggiore was to be built, financed by the patrician.

The altarpiece, of which a detail from the predella is illustrated here, represents the Madonna and Child enthroned with saints and angels. In the predella, composed of seven small scenes, are the events which led to the foundation of the Basilica by Pope Liberius. The simplicity of the portrayal, close to the frescoes of Masaccio and Masolino in the Carmine, is united with what has been defined as "the most radical experiment in realistic painting" of that time.

Paolo Veronese
Giuseppe da Porto with his Son Adrian

c. 1552-1553

Oil on canvas
247×137
Inv. Contini Bonacossi no. 16
In the Uffizi since 1998

Together with this portrait of himself with his son, Giuseppe da Porto, a noble man of Vicenza, commissioned Veronese to paint a similar portrait of his wife Livia Thiene with their daughter Porzia (Baltimore, Walters Art Gallery).

In the Uffizi painting, the father and the son are caught in a moment of affectionate embrace in a doorway.
The child's small hand is intertwined with the large hand of the father, who for this reason has taken off his glove.

Index